M000115394

UPTOWN DOWN SOUTH CUISINE

MAGNOLIAS RESTAURANT

DON DRAKE

Photographs by John D. Smoak III

GIBBS SMITH

TO ENRICH AND INSPIRE HUMANKIND

To everyone that has washed a dish,
chopped an onion, poured a drink,
taken an order and flipped a table.
I could not have done it without
each and every one of you
throughout the years.

To all the loyal patrons,
family and friends that have
and continue to support us.

To my sister Jo Ann,
who gave me my
first cookbook.

15 16 17 18 19   1 2 3 4 5
Text © 2015 Don Drake
and Hospitality Management Group, Inc
Photographs © 2015 John D. Smoak III

All rights reserved. No part of this book may be
reproduced by any means whatsoever without
written permission from the publisher, except
brief portions quoted for purpose of review.

Published by
Gibbs Smith
P.O. Box 667
Layton, Utah 84041

1.800.835.4993 orders
www.gibbs-smith.com

Designed by Katie Jennings Campbell
Page production by Renee Bond
Printed and bound in Hong Kong
Gibbs Smith books are printed on either recycled, 100%
post-consumer waste, FSC-certified papers or on paper produced
from a 100% certified sustainable forest/controlled wood source.

Library of Congress Cataloging-in-Publication Data

Drake, Don, 1960-
Uptown down South cuisine : Magnolias restaurant / Don Drake ; photo-
graphs by John D. Smoak III. — First edition.
    pages cm
Includes index.
ISBN 978-1-4236-3919-0
1. Cooking, American.—Southern style. 2. Cooking—South Carolina—
Charleston. 3. Magnolias (Restaurant) I. Magnolias (Restaurant) II. Title.
TX715.2.S68D73 2015
641.5975—dc23
                                           2014048821

CONTENTS

Acknowledgments

I WISH TO ACKNOWLEDGE THE FOLLOWING:

Suzi and T. J. Parsell for their encouragement, friendship and support in the project.

Mary Forlano for her endless hours deciphering my hieroglyphic writing, keeping me on track and assuring me the next one will be a piece of cake.

All the Magnolias alumni that contributed recipes for the book: Jeremy Ashby, Mark Graves, Ryan Dukes, Edwin French, Mike Dolberg, John Milner, Jeff Delmastro and Scott Popovic.

All the past and present chefs and sous chefs that helped Magnolias become the special place that the restaurant has evolved into the last 25 years: Donald Barickman, Casey Taylor, Cindy Ball, Gerald Mitchell, Glenn Swain, Frank Strauss, Mike Dragon, Brian Lyndsey, Norma Naparlo, Craig Deihl, John Milner, Katie Gulla, Adrian Pusser, Doug Beard, Kelly Franz, Kevin Southerland and James Simmons.

My present kitchen staff for holding the fort down while I was working on the project: Kelly, K-bone, James, Landice, Clarence, Sam and Ms. Marshall.

My pastry chef, Andrea Upchurch, who helped me through my shortcomings in the baking and pastry department.

John Smoak, our amazing photographer for this book.

Cathy Cuthbertson, a longtime family friend and copywriter/proofreader, who worked side by side with Mary to get this book done on time.

Our purveyors, whose answer is always, "Yes, we can get that," and dear friends: Andrea and Jack Limehouse from Limehouse Produce, Tony Ritter from US Foods, Dan Long from Crosby Seafood, and all our local farmers and fishmongers.

My wife, Martha, and my two sons, Marshall and Travis. I love you all very much. Thank you!

Foreword

IT WAS 1989, and the city of Charleston was recovering from the aftermath of the devastation of Hurricane Hugo when my late father, Tom Parsell, purchased an old historic building in the French Quarter District. In fact, it was the site of the city's original Customs House in 1739. Despite the Quarter having become a rundown part of town in the preceding years, he had a vision to reinvigorate the area with a traditional Lowcountry fine dining restaurant. Magnolias opened soon after that, in 1990, igniting a culinary renaissance and paving the way for restaurants in Charleston and across the South with its upscale southern cuisine. Likewise, Charleston itself has become a premier culinary destination in the South.

As I reflect on the past 25 years at Magnolias, I think of the history that has taken place in the restaurant—the countless meals we have provided for guests, the training given to young chefs chasing their dream, and the memorable experiences that we have created for those that have visited us. I have personally enjoyed many of those experiences over that time, including the marriage proposal to my wife, Louisa, as well as my family's annual Christmas Eve dinner. This cookbook celebrates those great meals, our loyal patrons and the unprecedented talent that has come through the kitchen—all of which have played a vital role in Magnolias' success.

How does a restaurant continue to be successful and relevant after two and a half decades? By providing the highest level of food and service day in, day out. We have been very fortunate to have had an incredible management team in place throughout the years to maintain that consistency. Since 1991, Executive Chef Don Drake has been the driving force behind Magnolias' ability to perpetuate the impeccable bar that has been set. His passion for food and hospitality continues to keep Magnolias at the top of its game, and I salute his dedication.

Chef Drake and I thought the 25th anniversary was the perfect time to refresh the restaurant space itself with a significant renovation to offer an updated environment with a new look. The dining room presents patrons with an enhanced experience complemented by the original southern charm for which Magnolias is best known. Similarly, we thought it was time for an updated cookbook. Inspired by Magnolias' original menu, this celebratory book features signature dishes from Chef Drake, as well as recipes from successful chefs that have spent time in Magnolias' kitchen. Our hope is that you will find recipes that will create as many special memories in your own kitchen as they have in ours.

—TJ Parsell, President/Owner
Hospitality Management Group, Inc.
Magnolias/Blossom/Cypress/Artisan Meat Share

Introduction

When it comes to cooking, my philosophy is straightforward: cooking shouldn't have a strict set of rules, and it should always be fun. I encourage you to play around and experiment with the recipes and ingredients, have fun with them. But I do have a few rules that will make a difference in every recipe you cook, from simple to complex.

Always use fresh produce and the freshest ingredients possible. It is a waste of your time, energy and money to use mediocre ingredients because the food you produce is only as good as what you started with, no matter how good the recipe.

Because acidic ingredients, such as vinegars or tomatoes, react with aluminum to create a metallic taste or discolored sauces, use cast iron pots and nonreactive mixing bowls and utensils for most of these recipes. (Non-reactive simply means that the bowl, pot or container contains no aluminum.)

Try to keep most of your pantry items in a cool, dry place, out of direct sunlight and away from heat.

If you're just learning how to cook, start out with the easier recipes and work your way up as you gain confidence in your skills. Cooking is like most other arts: the more you practice, the better your craft becomes.

I've grown accustomed to making big batches of food at Magnolias, so it's hard to make small batches when I'm at home. But if you're cooking just for two, go ahead and cut the recipe in half—that way you're not wasting anything. Finally, make sure you have enough time to enjoy the fruits of all the effort you put into making the meal. Slow down, pour a big glass of iced tea or open a bottle of wine, and savor the meal with family and friends.

Many of the basic ingredients in these recipes are found in the kitchens of most home cooks across the nation or are readily available at local grocers. Other products are regional in availability, but with the rise in popularity of the Southern Food movement, most can be found wherever you live.

Put on your apron. It's time to start cooking.

FROM THE SOUTHERN PANTRY

Nothing goes to waste in Magnolias' kitchen. I'm a little bit of a culinary packrat because I try to save everything: chicken bones, duck bones, shells from peeled shrimp, lobster shells, ham bones, vegetable scraps. They're all useful for making stocks, sauces and soups. If you have room in the freezer, wrap them up and freeze them for later. Things that seem like scraps will later add depth and flavor to all kinds of stocks.

When it comes to cooking, we frequently rely on descriptions borrowed from other languages and cultures. *Fond* is one such word, borrowed from French; it refers to the tasty little bits left at the bottom of a pan after something has been cooked. Using fonds is essential to creating flavorful stocks and sauces.

Looking at the big family tree of sauces and stocks, there are two grandparents. One is a *fond blanc* (white), the other, *fond brun* (brown). The bones in fond brun are roasted, whereas the bones in a fond blanc are not. A fond brun would be used for veal demi-glace or beef stock, and a fond blanc would be used for vegetable stock or shellfish and fish stocks. Either can be used for poultry stock.

Ratios for fonds and stocks are:
- 50% bones
- 10% mirepoix (a combination of onions, carrots and celery, chopped to about the size of a nickel)
- 40% enough water to cover

When making brown fonds or stocks, you'll sauté the mirepoix with the bones. To caramelize, add a little tomato paste, then add bay leaf, thyme and black peppercorns. Deglaze the pot with wine, using a red wine for darker sauces (fond brun) and a white wine for lighter sauces, scraping the bottom with a wooden spoon. Then add water to cover, letting it cook 2 hours for chicken, 45 minutes for shellfish or seafood, and about 3 hours for veal.

For a fond blanc or a white stock rinse your bones before cooking and sauté your vegetables just until softened but not browned. Then add herbs and peppercorns. Add wine if called for and enough cold water to cover.

Let's say the grandparents, fond blanc and fond brun, have five children and they are all women. They are known as mother sauces, or leading sauces, in the culinary world and are created by combining a liquid and a thickening agent.
- Milk + White Roux = Béchamel Sauce
- White Stock + White or Blond Roux = Velouté
- Brown Stock + Brown Roux = Espagnole
- Tomato + Stock = Tomato Sauce
- Butter + Eggs = Hollandaise

Think of all other sauces as distant cousins in the family tree. They are called small sauces and are all made from the mother sauces.

Roux is very basic but adds a great amount of flavor. Remember the ratio that works best is 1:1, meaning one part oil to one part flour. In a pan the size that suits your needs, heat the oil until it's very hot, then stir in an equal amount of flour. Use a large wooden spoon and try to stay away from rubber spoons when making roux, because the high temperature can cause them to melt. Reduce the heat and continue stirring until the roux reaches the color you are looking for—light roux for light sauces and darker colored for darker sauces. (The longer it cooks, the darker it becomes.) For instance, when I make gumbos I cook my roux until it turns medium brown. Then I add just the onions so they will caramelize. I don't add other vegetables until later on. They release too much water and deter browning, making it hard to get the dark chocolate color I need for a good gumbo base.

Chicken Stock

¹/₄ cup canola oil

1 medium to large onion, roughly chopped

1 carrot, peeled and roughly chopped

1 leek, white part only, roughly chopped

1 rib celery, roughly chopped

4 cloves garlic, crushed

1 pound roasted chicken bones or 1 ¹/₂ pounds rinsed chicken backs

1 dried bay leaf

4 sprigs fresh thyme

1 teaspoon black peppercorns

3 quarts water

Heat the canola oil in a large pot over moderate heat. Cook the onion, carrot, leek, celery and garlic, stirring often, until they are soft but not browned, about 4 minutes. Add the chicken bones and carcass, bay leaf, thyme, peppercorns and water. Increase the heat to high and bring to a boil, then reduce to low and simmer, skimming off any foam that rises to the surface. Continue cooking for about 2 hours, until the stock has reduced by half.

Strain the stock through a china cap or fine-mesh strainer. Allow the stock to chill in an ice bath. When the stock has cooled, skim the fat. It freezes well, so you can separate the stock and freeze it in small batches for future use.

VARIATIONS: To make fish stock, crab stock, or country ham or ham hock stock, substitute a seafood or ham protein of your choice for the chicken bones.

Veal Stock

1 pound veal bones

1/4 cup canola oil, divided

2 medium onions, chopped

1 carrot, peeled and chopped

1 rib celery, chopped

4 cloves garlic, crushed

1 leek, white part only, chopped

3 tablespoons tomato paste

750 ml red wine

1 dried bay leaf

3 sprigs fresh thyme

1 teaspoon black peppercorns

Preheat the oven to 450 degrees F.

Place veal bones in a roasting pan with sides, using half the oil to coat the bones. Roast the bones until well browned, about 45 minutes. Heat the remaining oil in a pot over medium-high heat. Add the onions and caramelize until they reach a dark brown color, about 10 minutes. Add carrot, celery, garlic, leek and tomato paste and cook for another 10 minutes, stirring often.

Add the veal bones to the pot, along with the wine, bay leaf, thyme and peppercorns. Add enough water to the pot to cover the bones, about 3 quarts. Bring to a boil, then turn down to a simmer. Skim off and discard the foam and any excessive amounts of fat that appears on top. Cook for about 2 hours, until the stock has reduced by half.

Strain stock through a fine sieve into a container with a lid, making sure to press all the juices from the vegetables. Allow to cool. Once the stock has chilled, the fat will solidify on top and you can easily scrape it off and discard. Divide into small batches and refrigerate for up to 2 weeks or freeze for up to 3 months.

Shellfish Stock

Makes 6 cups

1/4 cup canola oil

1 medium to large onion, roughly chopped

1 rib celery, roughly chopped

1 carrot, peeled and roughly chopped

1 leek, white part only, roughly chopped

4 cloves garlic, crushed

3 sprigs fresh tarragon

6 fresh basil leaves

1 teaspoon black peppercorns

1 dried bay leaf

Shells from 3 large lobsters, crushed
   or 1 pound shrimp shells, crushed

1 (6-ounce) can tomato paste

1 cup brandy

8 cups water or reserved liquid from cooking the
   lobster

Heat the canola oil in a large pot over moderate heat. Cook the onion, celery, carrot, leek and garlic, stirring often, until soft but not brown, about 4 minutes. Add tarragon, basil, black peppercorns, bay leaf, and crushed lobster or shrimp shells. Add tomato paste and stir to coat the shells. Continue to cook until the tomato paste has darkened a little, then deglaze the pan with brandy and reduce the liquid by half, about 5 minutes. Add your water or liquid from cooking the lobsters. Bring to a simmer; remove and discard any impurities that might have risen to the top. Simmer for 35 minutes. Chill well, then place in small containers and freeze for up to 3 months or refrigerate for up to 1 week.

Trinity

Makes 3 cups

Trinity consists of onions, celery and bell peppers. In southern Creole cuisine, this flavorful combination is referred to as the Holy Trinity, and rightly so. It is the foundation of a multitude of dishes, from gumbo to étouffée.

1 tablespoon olive oil

2 cups diced yellow onion

2 cups chopped celery

1 cup diced red bell pepper

In a heavy-bottomed 12-inch skillet over medium-low heat, add the olive oil and sauté all ingredients until soft and just beginning to caramelize, about 15 minutes.

If making trinity for chicken or roasted Creole dishes, heat the oil and sauté the onions until caramelized, about 10 minutes. Add the celery and bell peppers and sauté for another 5 minutes, adding about 1/8 cup water. Turn the heat to low and cook for another 20 minutes, stirring often. The mixture will be a golden brown.

Grilled Sweet Corn Relish

Makes 3 cups

8 ears corn on the cob, shucked

7 tablespoons extra virgin olive oil

$^1/_4$ cup finely diced red onion

$^1/_4$ cup finely diced red bell pepper

$^1/_2$ cup thinly sliced green onion

1 teaspoon chopped garlic

2 teaspoons seeded and minced jalapeño

1 tablespoon chopped cilantro

4 tablespoons apple cider vinegar

1 teaspoon ground cumin

1 teaspoon coarse sea salt

$^1/_2$ teaspoon freshly ground black pepper

Start the grill. When the fire is hot, rub each corn on the cob with 1 tablespoon of olive oil and place the corn on the hot grill. Grill until slightly charred. Allow to cool. Using a sharp knife cut the kernels off the cob, place them in a medium-sized bowl and mix with the remaining ingredients. Store in airtight container and refrigerate for up to 1 week.

You can pretty much can and pickle almost any kind of food. At Magnolias we mostly preserve vegetables and fruits, extending the spring and summer seasons to enjoy later. I'm a big fan of pickled fruits and vegetables, and preserving has been popular in southern cuisine since the invention of glass. Most of the containers we use are common Mason jars. They've been around for many years. A lot of hardware stores carry them, and they cost a lot less than the ones you'll find at fashionable culinary stores. If you have enough room to store the jars, buy them by the dozen, and they will be cheaper. Besides, there aren't any recipes I know of that only yield one jar of preserved fruits or vegetables, so you'll need a few jars on hand.

I usually use a hot-water bath rather than a pressure canner because most of the things I preserve are acidic, like pickles, preserves, chutneys, relishes and chow-chows. When you deal with low-acid items, like seafood, meats, vegetables, and poultry, you need to use a pressure canner to get the temperature up to 240 degrees F to kill all the bacteria.

HOT-WATER BATH METHOD

First, assemble all of your supplies: glass jars (mostly pints and quarts), caps and bands, and a large stock pot that will hold a rack in the bottom (or use a boiling-water canner). Jars can't rest on the bottom of the pot because they'll burst. You'll need a pot that is deep and wide enough to cover the jars with an inch or two of water. You'll also need measuring cups and spoons, a wide-mouth funnel, a chopstick for air pockets, a jar lifter, a set of tongs, clean dish towels and a ladle.

Once you've gathered your equipment, inspect the caps and screw-on bands for damage, and heat the oven to 200 degrees F. Place the jars in the stock pot or canner on their sides, and fill the pot with enough water to cover the jars by at least 1 to 2 inches. Bring to a boil and then reduce to a simmer. Remove the jars, tilting slightly to let the water run back into the pot. Place jars in a large roasting pan and put them in the preheated oven until ready for use.

In a small pot bring some water to a boil, then reduce heat to a simmer and add the bands and caps. Do not boil the caps. Let the bands and caps sit in the water until ready to use. Carefully remove the jars from the oven, placing the jars and the stock pot on a flat surface. Use the wide-mouth funnel to fill the jars, allowing for headspace as directed in the recipes. Carefully remove the funnel and use the chopstick to remove any visible air pockets. When the jars are filled, wipe clean the jar rims, and remove the caps from the water using a set of small tongs. Place caps on the center of the jars, then remove the bands from the water and tighten on firmly, finger tight. You want exhaust air to be able to escape. Fill and cap all jars. If you have a jar lifter, use it to lower the jars carefully into the water bath so that each jar is submerged and covered. Bring the water to a boil, and process according to the recipe.

Carefully remove the jars from the water and set them on a clean dish towel to cool. Wipe the water from the lids, but try not to disturb the contents. As the jars cool, the lids will get sucked down, creating a seal. Some will pop, some will not, and you will be able to see if a jar has not sealed. Let jars sit for 6 to 8 hours and cool to room temperature. They are now ready to store. If the jar failed to seal, reprocess it or refrigerate and use within 1 year.

PRESSURE CANNING METHOD

Pressure canning is a lot like the procedure above, except the temperature requirements are different. Water boils at 212 degrees F, and in a hot-water bath temperatures run between 180 and 212 degrees F. For low-acid canning, the temperature has to reach a minimum of 240 degrees F to avoid clostridium botulinum and its mold-producing spores, which lead to botulism. To kill the spores, the product has to be cooked for the required amount of time at 240 degrees F or higher. Here's a quick run-through.

Cook the product according to the recipe you're using, and follow all the steps for the hot-water bath method to the point of placing the filled jars in the stock pot. Prepare your pressure canner by filling it with 3 to 4 inches of water, or an amount that fulfills the manufacturer's guidelines. Place the jars in the pressure canner and lock the pressure canner lid in place, leaving the vent pipe open. Allow steam to vent for 8 to 10 minutes to make sure there is no air and only steam left. Close the vent and process for the amount of time indicated in the recipe you're using. Adjust the heat during the cooking to maintain the recommended amount of pressure as needed.

When the processing time is up, remove from heat. Don't touch the vent; let the pressure return to zero on its own. Follow the manufacturer's instructions, and allow 10 minutes after it has returned to zero before opening the canner. Carefully open the lid, making sure the lid faces away from you so that steam is directed away from you. Wait 10 minutes more, and then remove the hot jars and transfer them to a dish towel on the counter. Let the jars sit on the counter undisturbed for 12 hours. Check the lids for a good seal. If you can't pop them with your fingertip, you're good to go. Store in a cupboard or other cool, dry spot away from heat sources.

Finally, make sure to date and label the products. Have you ever been to someone's basement or garage with canned goods everywhere and no date or label on anything? You never know how old the stuff is. Don't be one of those people! Date and label everything. Canned goods usually have a 1-year shelf life. If anything is a year old, get rid of it.

Chow-Chow

Makes 2 quarts

3 pounds green tomatoes, cored and chopped

1 red bell pepper, seeded and chopped

1 green bell pepper, seeded and chopped

1 head green cabbage, shredded

3 jalapeño peppers, seeded and chopped

3 cups apple cider vinegar

1 1/2 cups sugar

1/4 cup prepared horseradish

1 tablespoon mustard seeds

1/4 teaspoon ground cloves

1 tablespoon ground cinnamon

1/2 teaspoon ground allspice

1 tablespoon coarse sea salt

In a large pot over high heat, combine all the ingredients and bring to a boil. Reduce the heat to a simmer and cook for 45 minutes to 1 hour, stirring occasionally. Most of the liquid should evaporate and the mixture should be thick.

Remove the pot from the heat. Divide the mixture between 2 sterilized (1-quart) jars and seal immediately (see "Canning, Pickling and Putting Up" on page 14).

Peach Chutney

Makes 3 cups

4 cups peeled, roughly chopped peaches, fresh or frozen

1 cup minced yellow onion

2 tablespoons peeled, finely minced ginger

1 cup finely diced red bell pepper

1 cup sugar

1/4 cup apple cider vinegar

In a heavy-bottomed pot over medium-high heat, place all of the ingredients and stir well to combine. Reduce the heat to a simmer and cook for 25 to 30 minutes, stirring occasionally, until the peach chutney begins to thicken slightly. Use right away, or chill and store in an airtight container and refrigerate for up to 2 weeks.

Bread-and-Butter Pickles

Makes 2 1/2 gallons

36 cucumbers, cut into 1/3-inch-thick slices

8 small Vidalia or yellow onions, thinly sliced

1 red bell pepper, seeded and thinly sliced

1 cup coarse sea salt

10 cups white vinegar

10 cups sugar

4 tablespoons brown mustard seeds

1 teaspoon turmeric

1 teaspoon ground cloves

2 teaspoons celery seeds

In a large perforated pan, mix together the cucumbers, onions, red pepper and salt; allow to sit for 2 hours.

In a large pot, combine the vinegar, sugar, mustard seeds, turmeric, cloves and celery seeds; bring to a boil.

Meanwhile, rinse the cucumber mixture well with cold water. Add the cucumber mixture to the boiling brine. As soon as the brine begins to boil again, remove the pot from the heat right away. Transfer the mixture into 1 large airtight container or several sterilized jars (see "Canning, Pickling and Putting Up" on page 14) and refrigerate until cool.

Roasted Garlic Purée

Makes $^1/_2$ to $^2/_3$ cup

The easiest way to make roasted garlic is on a sheet tray with raised sides, using cloves that have already been peeled. Peeled garlic cloves are readily available in the produce section of most grocery stores; they're sold in bags, cartons or plastic containers. This purée freezes well.

2 cups whole peeled cloves garlic

$^1/_4$ cup olive oil

Salt and pepper

Preheat oven to 375 degrees.

In a baking pan, ovenproof dish or sheet tray with sides, spread out the garlic cloves and drizzle with olive oil. Add enough water to the pan to cover the garlic. Place in the preheated oven and bake for 25 minutes, or until the water has evaporated and the garlic cloves are golden brown and soft. Remove the pan from the oven and purée the garlic in a food processor. Season with salt and pepper to taste. Store in an airtight container and refrigerate for up to 2 weeks.

Scented Sugars

Scented sugars have many uses, from making cakes, frostings, jams and preserves to making your favorite cocktails and hot toddies. Just make sure the jars and plant materials are clean and dry. Some of our favorite scented sugars used in the restaurant are made with dried fruits and herbs, most of which can be purchased at larger grocery stores.

VANILLA SUGAR

3 vanilla beans, halved lengthwise

3 pounds granulated or powdered sugar

CHOCOLATE-VANILLA SUGAR

3 vanilla beans, halved lengthwise

1 cup cocoa

3 pounds granulated or powdered sugar

ORANGE-CINNAMON SUGAR

1 1/2 cups sugar

2 tablespoons ground cinnamon

2 tablespoons dried grated orange peel

STRAWBERRY-BANANA SUGAR

1 1/2 cups sugar

1/4 cup freeze-dried strawberry pieces

1/4 cup dried banana chips, whole

LEMON SUGAR

1 1/2 cups sugar

2 tablespoons dried grated lemon peel

COCONUT SUGAR

1 1/2 cups sugar

1/3 cup unsweetened coconut flakes

LAVENDER SUGAR

1 1/2 cups sugar

3 tablespoons lavender

CRÈME BRÛLÉE SUGAR

1 1/2 cups sugar

1 1/2 cups firmly packed light brown sugar

APPLE-CINNAMON SUGAR

1 1/2 cups sugar

1/4 cup dried apples, ground

2 tablespoons ground cinnamon

JALAPEÑO-LIME SUGAR

1 1/2 cups sugar

2 tablespoons dried ground jalapeños

2 tablespoons dried ground lime peel

To make each recipe, simply combine all ingredients and store in an airtight container at a cool room temperature.

SAUCES, SPICES, RUBS & MARINADES

Barbecue Dry Rub

Makes 4 ¼ cups

This combination comes from Magnolias alumnus Jeff Delmastro.

1 cup smoked paprika

1 cup granulated garlic

1 tablespoon ground ginger

1 teaspoon ground celery seed

1 teaspoon freshly ground black pepper

1 teaspoon crushed red pepper flakes

1 teaspoon onion powder

1 teaspoon dry mustard

1 teaspoon dried thyme

½ teaspoon cayenne

¼ cup kosher salt

1 cup firmly packed brown sugar

Combine all the ingredients and mix well. Store in an airtight container or ziplock bag.

Steak Seasoning

Makes ¾ cup

2 tablespoons kosher salt

2 tablespoons cracked pepper

2 tablespoons smoked paprika

1 tablespoon granulated garlic

1 tablespoon granulated onion

1 tablespoon ground coriander seed

1 tablespoon crushed red pepper flakes

Measure and mix all seasonings together. Store in an airtight container.

Grilled or Roasted Chicken Rub

Makes ³/₄ cup

Rub the bird earlier in the day and let it sit to absorb the flavor. Make sure to season the cavity if roasting it whole.

2 tablespoons dried thyme

2 tablespoons dried oregano

2 tablespoons ground cumin

2 tablespoons paprika

2 teaspoons onion powder

2 teaspoons dried sage

¹/₂ teaspoon salt

¹/₂ teaspoon ground black pepper

Combine all the ingredients and mix well. Store in an airtight container.

Magnolias Southern Blackening Spice

Makes 1¹/₃ cups

6 tablespoons smoked paprika

2 teaspoons coarse sea salt

2 tablespoons granulated onion

2 teaspoons ground black pepper

2 teaspoons cayenne pepper

2 teaspoons ground thyme

2 teaspoons dried oregano

1 teaspoon granulated garlic

1 tablespoon chile powder

1 tablespoon ground cumin

Measure and mix all seasonings together. Store in an airtight container.

Creole Seasoning

Makes 1 cup

4 tablespoons celery salt

2 tablespoons paprika

2 tablespoons coarse sea salt

2 tablespoons ground black pepper

2 tablespoons granulated onion

2 tablespoons granulated garlic

4 teaspoons cayenne pepper

1 teaspoon ground allspice

Combine all the ingredients and mix well. Store in an airtight container.

Sweet Potato Hot Sauce

Makes 7 cups

My good friends from St. Augustine, Tracy and Angie Geiger, moved to St. Thomas in the U.S. Virgin Islands about 18 years ago. On a trip down there, Tracy took my son and me on a weeklong sailing adventure through the British Virgin Islands. While we were island hopping we stopped at a local sandwich spot for a bite to eat. A bottle of hot sauce on the table caught my eye, and we had to sample some. The guy serving us said it was a carrot hot sauce. I thought it was mighty tasty. It had great flavor and didn't burn you up. I decided to put a southern twist on it using sweet potatoes, so here it is. Give it a try. If you want more heat, add more peppers. Exercise caution when handling hot peppers. Wear latex gloves and be careful not to touch your face or eyes. Adjust the flavor with more salt, sugar or cayenne as desired.

1 small sweet potato, diced

1 carrot, peeled and diced

1 yellow onion, diced

6 Fresno chiles or Dutch reds, stemmed and seeded

2 habanero chiles, stemmed and seeded

5 cloves garlic, crushed and minced

Pinch of ground cumin

2 cups distilled vinegar

2 cups water

1 tablespoon coarse sea salt

1 teaspoon sugar

1 teaspoon molasses

In a medium-sized pot, combine all the ingredients and bring to a slow rolling boil. Cover and cook for 30 minutes. Remove the pot from the heat and allow the mixture to cool. Purée the mixture in a blender, then strain for a smoother sauce. Store in an airtight container and refrigerate for up to 3 months.

Tartar Sauce

Makes 1 3/4 cups

Tartar sauce is great with seafood of all kinds.

1 1/4 cups Duke's mayonnaise

1/3 cup pickle relish (hot, sweet or dill)

2 tablespoons capers, rinsed and chopped

1 hard-boiled egg, finely chopped

Dash of Frank's RedHot sauce

Dash of Worcestershire sauce

Coarse sea salt

White pepper

In a medium-sized bowl combine the mayonnaise, relish, capers and egg; mix well. Add the Frank's RedHot and Worcestershire sauces, check for seasoning, stir well and chill. Store in an airtight container and refrigerate for up to 1 week.

South Carolina Mustard Sauce

Makes 11 cups

Barbecue master Jeff Delmastro contributed this recipe.

1 quart French's mustard

1 quart Heinz apple cider vinegar

2 tablespoons ground black pepper

2 tablespoons dark chili powder

5 tablespoons granulated garlic

2 tablespoons crushed red pepper flakes

3/4 cup Worcestershire sauce

3 tablespoons kosher salt

1 1/2 pounds brown sugar

In a medium-size saucepan, combine all the ingredients and bring to a simmer over low heat. Cook for 15 minutes, stirring occasionally. Remove from heat and allow sauce to cool. Store in an airtight container and refrigerate for up to 3 months.

BREAD, BISCUITS & GRAVIES

Buttermilk Biscuits

Makes 1 dozen biscuits

2 cups whole-wheat flour

2 teaspoons baking powder

$^1/_2$ teaspoon baking soda

$^1/_2$ teaspoon salt (optional)

5 teaspoons salted butter

$^3/_4$ cup buttermilk

1 tablespoon butter, melted

Preheat the oven to 450 degrees F.

Sift together all dry ingredients in a mixing bowl. Cut in the butter until pea-sized pieces form, and mix until it resembles a coarse meal. Make a well in the middle of the mixture and pour in the buttermilk. Stir until a soft dough is formed, but be careful not to overmix it. Turn the dough out onto a floured surface and knead for about 1 minute. Pat or roll out the dough to $^3/_4$-inch thickness. Use a biscuit cutter or water glass to cut the dough into 2-inch rounds. Place the rounds on a greased baking tray and brush with butter. Bake for 12 to 15 minutes.

Grit Biscuits

Makes 2 dozen biscuits

During 25 years of cooking grits, we've made Christmas grit cookies, grit flatbread, grit crackers, grit cheese thins. You name it and we've probably tried it once or twice.

2 cups milk

2 teaspoons coarse sea salt

$^1/_2$ cup molasses

$^1/_2$ cup stone-ground grits

$^1/_4$ cup lukewarm water

1 package (2 $^1/_4$ teaspoons) active dry yeast

2 large eggs, beaten

2 cups whole-wheat flour

$^1/_2$ cup margarine, cut into cubes

2 cups White Lily Self-Rising flour, divided

In a medium-sized saucepot, bring the milk, salt and molasses to a boil. Slowly stir in the grits. Allow the mixture to return to a boil, then reduce to a simmer and cook for 40 minutes. Remove from heat and allow to cool.

In a stand mixer fitted with a paddle, combine the water and yeast and let dissolve. Add the grits and eggs and beat for 60 seconds. Add whole-wheat flour and cut in the margarine. Change the fitted paddle to a dough hook and add the White Lily flour.

Knead the dough until it forms a soft ball. Place in a greased bowl and gently turn the dough to coat both sides with a little of the oil in the bowl. Cover with a towel or wrap in plastic. Place in a warm spot to rise until the dough doubles in volume. Punch down the dough. On a floured surface, roll the dough to a 1-inch thickness and cut into rounds with a biscuit cutter. Place the rounds onto a greased baking pan, and preheat the oven to 375 degrees F. Let the dough rise for 30 minutes. Bake for 15 to 20 minutes, or until browned.

We use a lot of different varieties of sandwich breads, rolls, biscuits, cornbreads and muffins at the restaurant. But when it comes right down to, it all breads share the same common denominators: a baked dough of flour and water, leavened by yeast. Other recipes add cornmeal, sugar, shortening, eggs and flavorings, but flour, water and yeast are the building blocks.

Most bread making involves a 12-step process: measuring, mixing, fermentation, punching, scaling, rounding, benching, panning, proofing, baking, cooling and storing. It looks like a long list, but after a few tries it becomes a simple pattern. In culinary school they try to drill this process into your head, but a lot of non-bakers and pastry majors had to take an extra baking class. I love baking, but I do wish I had paid more attention!

Cornbread

Makes one 9-inch skillet

For something as simple as cornbread, there's a surprising amount of conflict between those on the north and south sides of the Mason–Dixon Line. No self-respecting southerner would put sugar in their cornbread, because if God had meant cornbread to have sugar in it, he'd have called it cake. Some true purists don't use any flour either. People from certain areas believe yellow corn is animal feed, so they eat only white corn. However you eat cornbread, it's always a treat. I remember my mother pouring a big glass of buttermilk, putting cornbread fresh out of the oven right into the glass and then eating it with a spoon. What makes really great cornbread is the crust, and the trick is to use a hot, seasoned 9-inch cast iron pan and bacon drippings (you can use butter if it makes you feel better).

1/4 cup plus 2 tablespoons bacon drippings

1 cup medium-grind white or yellow cornmeal

1 cup White Lily Self-Rising flour

2/3 cup sugar

1/2 teaspoon salt

3 1/2 teaspoons baking powder

2 eggs

1 1/4 cup buttermilk

Preheat the oven to 450 degrees F. Pour 2 tablespoons bacon drippings into a 9-inch cast iron skillet and put the skillet into the oven.

In a large mixing bowl, combine the cornmeal, flour, sugar, salt and baking powder. In a small bowl, add the eggs, buttermilk and remaining 1/4 cup bacon drippings; mix well. Pour the egg mixture into the cornmeal mixture and mix well. Remove the hot skillet from the oven and pour the mixture into the skillet. Return the skillet to the oven and bake the cornbread until golden brown and firm in the middle, about 15 to 20 minutes.

{ VERSATILE CORNMEAL }

When it comes to the South, one particular food item that separates us from other parts of the country is corn. It's around in every form—fresh, dried and distilled. Corn is prevalent in the South because of its availability and low cost. It has been used since forever in place of wheat, which doesn't grow in the South. We have our cornbreads, hushpuppies, spoon breads, fritters, dumplings, pone and dog bread.

Cornmeal for cornbread usually comes in two varieties or colors: white and yellow. I prefer white corn over yellow corn because I think it has a higher sugar content, but you be the judge. What matters most when choosing cornmeal is the freshness rather than the color. Seek out corn that has just been milled. You will be amazed by the difference in quality and taste.

Fresh out of the oven with some butter, skillet cornbread is king. There are many variations of this southern standard. Some call for sugar and others add not a speck. Some of the mountain people in the uplands of the Carolinas make a gritted cornbread late into the corn season after the grains have hardened. Hushpuppies—a cornbread hybrid if ever there was one—were tossed to the dogs to keep them fed and quiet. The humble beginnings of cornbread and hushpuppies were nothing more than fat and cornmeal rolled up and cooked over the fire on the flat end of a hoe (hoe cake). But hushpuppies are mainstream now and filled with various items. I usually cook my hushpuppies right after I have fried my seafood so the oil will add a little seafood flavor to the dough.

Cornbread and hushpuppies may be the most common of the cornmeal concoctions, but there are several other favorites. Spoon breads are a southern version of a soufflé. (I share two different versions in this cookbook, one that uses egg whites and one that does not.) Hoe cakes are a combination of dog bread and spoon bread, more like a southern pancake. They go great with varied items from seafood to grilled chicken. Quite often we serve them on the Magnolias menu as a starch or side dish.

Pone and dog bread are the most basic of cornbreads, and mostly consist of cornmeal, salt, grease and hot water. Our southern pone and dog bread are sort of like England's Yorkshire puddings. They go great with roasts of all kinds and are equally good with potlikker. Don't quote me on this, but I believe the difference between the two is that corn pone is made with white cornmeal, salt, bacon fat, and boiling water. Dog bread is made from cornmeal, salt and cold water mixed together and allowed to sit. It's shaped into thin biscuits and fried in bacon fat.

Jalapeño Cornbread

This is an old recipe out of the family recipe index card holder. A lot of the handwritten ones are getting harder to read as the years go by. I really need to make a digital copy to save for the kids. The jalapeños pack a little heat here, but it's quite moderate and not too hot. We use this bread in a lot of different ways, from sandwiches to croutons to spoon breads.

1 cup stone-ground whole-wheat flour

2 1/2 cups medium grind yellow cornmeal

1 tablespoon honey

1 tablespoon sea salt

4 teaspoons aluminum-free baking powder

1 teaspoon baking soda

3 large eggs, beaten

1 1/2 cups buttermilk, room temperature

1/2 cup canola oil

1 (15-ounce) can creamed corn, or 1 3/4 cups creamed corn (see page 170)

6 jalapeño peppers, seeded and diced

1 large yellow onion, grated

2 1/2 cups grated Cracker Barrel sharp yellow cheddar cheese

Preheat the oven to 425 degrees F. Grease three 8 x 4-inch loaf pans and set aside.

In a bowl, combine the flour, cornmeal, honey, sea salt, baking powder and baking soda.

In another bowl, combine the eggs, buttermilk, and canola oil and mix well. Add the liquid mixture to the first bowl and stir in the creamed corn, jalapeños, onion, and cheese, mixing well after each addition. Pour the batter into the loaf pans, dividing equally. Bake for 35 to 40 minutes, until a toothpick comes out clean and dry. Let the bread cool in the pans before turning out onto a rack or towel to cool. Serve with salted butter.

No-Flour, No-Sugar Cornbread—
The Real Thing

Makes one 9-inch skillet

4 tablespoons bacon drippings

2 cups white cornmeal

$1/2$ teaspoon baking powder

$1/2$ teaspoon baking soda

1 teaspoon salt

1 egg

$1 1/2$ cups buttermilk

Preheat the oven to 450 degrees. Pour the bacon drippings into a 9-inch cast iron skillet and put the skillet into the oven.

In a large mixing bowl, combine the cornmeal, baking powder, baking soda and salt. Add the egg and buttermilk and mix just until blended.

Remove the hot skillet from the oven, and carefully pour the bacon drippings into the cornbread batter. Quickly mix the batter, then pour the batter back into the skillet and return it to the hot oven. Cook for about 20 to 25 minutes, until firm in the middle. Turn the cornbread out onto a big plate. It should slide right out of the pan.

Cornbread Croutons

Makes about 30 croutons

Cornbread croutons are a delicious combination of crunchy and chewy in one bite. They add extra flavor and texture to a salad or soup, and they are simple to make, using any of the cornbread recipes in the book. These croutons are best made with day-old cornbread that has dried out a bit.

1 (9 x 13-inch pan) day-old cornbread (see cornmeal muffin recipe, page 35)

$1/4$ cup olive oil

$1/2$ teaspoon sea salt

$1/4$ teaspoon freshly ground black pepper

If you're making the cornbread fresh, bake according to directions, allow to cool, and then slice into bite-sized pieces about $3/4$ x $3/4$-inch thick. Place on a sheet tray to dry out overnight.

Preheat the oven to 350 degrees.

Place the cornbread into a bowl big enough to hold the pieces, and lightly coat with olive oil. Add a sprinkle of salt and pepper, and place the pieces on a baking tray or sheet pan. Bake for

7 to 10 minutes, or until they are toasted golden brown. The croutons will keep for a couple of days in an airtight container.

JALAPEÑO CORNBREAD CROUTONS VARIATION: Use about 25 slices of cooled Jalapeño Cornbread (see page 30), sliced into $3/4$-inch-thick pieces (form slices, not cubes). Dry out overnight, lightly coat both sides with olive oil, salt and pepper, and cook as above.

Corn Pone Bread

This dish has been around since colonial times. Now it's making a comeback.

Bacon drippings

1 1/2 cups cornmeal

1/2 cup unbleached all-purpose flour

1/2 teaspoon coarse sea salt

2 1/2 cups boiling water

1 1/2 cups molasses

2 tablespoons honey

4 tablespoons butter, melted

Preheat the oven to 375 degrees F. Grease a 10-inch cast iron skillet with bacon drippings and put the skillet into the oven.

In a large bowl, sift together the cornmeal, flour and salt. Pour in the boiling water and mix well.

Add the molasses, honey, and butter and mix again. Remove the hot skillet from the oven. Pour the mixture into in the hot skillet and return it to the oven. Bake for 15 minutes. Flip the pone, put a cover on top, and bake for 5 to 10 minutes more, until bread has a semi-firm texture.

Dog Bread

Makes 13 to 15 cakes

This is an old-fashioned style of bread in its simplest form.

1 1/2 cups bacon drippings

1 cup cornmeal

1/4 teaspoon salt

1 cup water

In a medium-sized cast iron skillet, heat the bacon drippings over medium heat.

In a small bowl, combine the cornmeal and salt, mixing well. Add the water and stir until the mixture becomes a thick batter. Let it sit for 2 minutes.

Using 2 spoons—one to scoop and one to scrape because the batter will be tacky—form 3 little silver dollar pancakes by dropping batter into the hot bacon grease. Fry until golden brown. Place on a brown paper bag and keep warm. Repeat until all the batter is used. Serve hot with salted butter.

Spoon Bread

Makes one 9-inch skillet or 12 ramekins

If you do not have buttermilk, substitute sour cream or whole milk, but add 2 teaspoons of vinegar for every cup of milk.

3 cups milk

3 cups buttermilk

2 cups medium grind cornmeal

1 tablespoon sea salt

1/4 cup bacon drippings or melted butter

2 tablespoons sugar

6 egg yolks, beaten

1 cup chopped fresh herbs (such as chives, basil, chervil)

6 egg whites, stiffly beaten

1 1/2 tablespoons baking powder

Preheat the oven to 350 degrees F. Grease your skillet or ramekins with butter, then dust with cornmeal and set aside in a cool place.

In a medium-sized saucepot, bring milk and buttermilk to a boil. Pull from the heat and immediately whisk the cornmeal into the milk in a slow, steady stream, paying particular attention not to allow the mixture to get too lumpy. Add the salt, drippings or butter, sugar, egg yolks, and herbs and mix well. Using a large spoon, add a spoonful of the whipped egg whites to the cornmeal mixture to loosen it up. Gently fold in the remaining egg whites and the baking powder with a rubber spatula. Ladle the dough into your prepared pan or ramekins. Place in a water bath and bake for 35 minutes. Check with a toothpick. Spoon bread should have the consistency of a pudding-style cornbread.

Old-School Grated-Corn Spoon Bread

Makes 6–8 servings

This recipe takes us back to the days when regular white milk was called "sweet milk." Maybe a few of you still remember those days. You won't find any whipped egg whites in this recipe, no sir.

2 ears of corn

1 cup boiling water

1/2 cup cornmeal

1/2 cup milk

3/4 teaspoon salt

1/4 teaspoon freshly ground black pepper

1 1/2 teaspoons baking powder

1 tablespoon butter, softened

2 eggs, beaten

3 tablespoons bacon drippings

Cut the kernels off the cob and grate the corn ears to get the remaining corn milk off the cob. Preheat the oven to 400 degrees F.

Pour the boiling water over the cornmeal and beat in the milk, salt, pepper, baking powder, butter and eggs. Grease a 1-quart baking dish with the bacon drippings, and sprinkle the corn into the dish. Pour the liquid mixture into the dish. Bake for 20 minutes, or until set. Serve warm with butter.

Cornmeal Muffins

Makes 12

If you do not have buttermilk, substitute sour cream or whole milk, but add 2 teaspoons of vinegar for every cup of milk. If you're making cornbread croutons, this recipe can be used to make a 9 x 13-inch pan of cornbread.

2 tablespoons bacon drippings

1 cup medium-grind cornmeal

3 cups all-purpose flour

1 cup sugar

1 teaspoon coarse sea salt

1 1/2 tablespoons baking powder

4 eggs, beaten

2 1/2 cups buttermilk

1 cup melted butter

Preheat the oven to 350 degrees F. Grease a 12-cup muffin tin with bacon drippings and set aside.

In a large mixing bowl, sift together the cornmeal, flour, sugar, salt and baking powder. Stir in the eggs, buttermilk and butter. Mix well and pour into the greased muffin cups. Bake for 15 to 20 minutes, or until golden brown.

It's sometimes called slider sauce at my house. It slides in and slides out, pan-to-plate and, boy, is it good. Pan gravies are incorporated into the heart and soul of southern cooking, from fried chicken and country-fried steak to smothered pork chops and biscuits and gravy. We love it. So will you.

BASIC PAN GRAVY

Choose your meat and brown it off in a heavy skillet. After the meat is nicely cooked and browned, pour off the drippings into a heatproof cup and save for later. Don't clean and scrape the skillet, but let the crumbs and sprinkles remain. Return the skillet to the stove, and over medium heat add grease or pan drippings. Sprinkle the flour over the hot drippings, whisking constantly to prevent lumps. If it looks too oily, add more flour. If it looks a little too thick or lumpy, add more drippings. Cook it to the color you desire. Add milk or stock, whisking constantly until the gravy is smooth and thick, about 8 to 10 minutes. Make sure the gravy is well seasoned with cracked black pepper and a little salt. Keep warm.

Sausage Biscuit Gravy

Makes 2 1/2 cups

1 pound mild breakfast sausage

3 tablespoons all-purpose flour

2 cups milk

1/2 teaspoon cracked black pepper

Fry the sausage in a large cast iron skillet until it's browned and crumbled. Remove the sausage from the skillet and pour off all drippings except about 3 tablespoons. Slowly add the flour to the drippings, whisking to prevent any lumps. Cook for about 1 minute over medium heat, and gradually add milk until it reaches the thickness you desire. Stir the pepper and the cooked sausage into the smooth gravy. Serve with piping hot biscuits

Fried Chicken Gravy

Makes 3 cups

1 cup mild bulk sausage

$^1/_4$ cup diced yellow onion

2 tablespoons finely diced red pepper

1 rib celery, diced

$^1/_4$ cup all-purpose flour

5 cups chicken stock, plus more if needed

$^1/_2$ cup heavy cream or milk

1 dried bay leaf

1 teaspoon Kitchen Bouquet browning and seasoning sauce

1 teaspoon chopped fresh sage

Salt and pepper

Fry the chicken in a skillet large enough to give the pieces plenty of room to brown evenly. After the chicken is finished frying, pour off all but $^1/_4$ cup oil out of the pan. Brown the sausage, breaking it up as it cooks. Add the onion, red pepper and celery and sauté until the vegetables are soft. Sprinkle in the flour and stir until well combined. Stir in the chicken stock, heavy cream or milk, bay leaf, Kitchen Bouquet, and sage and cook for 10 minutes on medium-low heat. Add more chicken stock if needed to thin out the gravy. Season to taste with salt and pepper.

APPETIZERS

Deviled Crab Backs

Makes 1 dozen

1/4 cup diced red onion

1/4 cup diced celery

1/2 cup diced red pepper

1/2 cup diced green pepper

1/2 cup chopped fresh parsley

1 pound lump crabmeat

1/2 cup whole grain mustard

1/4 cup mayonnaise

1/4 teaspoon celery seed

1/2 teaspoon coarse sea salt

1/4 teaspoon Tabasco sauce

1 teaspoon Worcestershire sauce

1/2 cup grated Parmesan cheese

1/4 cup grated yellow cheddar cheese

3 eggs, beaten

2/3 cup panko bread crumbs

1/4 cup butter, melted

1/2 cup all-purpose flour

1 1/2 cups heavy cream

Creole rémoulade sauce (recipe follows)

Prepare 12 crab backs, or a buttered 8 x 8-inch baking dish.

In a medium-sized bowl, combine all ingredients except the butter, flour, cream, and Rémoulade Sauce and mix well. Preheat the oven to 425 degrees F.

In a small saucepan over medium heat, melt the butter and stir in the flour, making a blond roux.

Cook for 2 minutes. Add the cream, whisking constantly to prevent lumps. Cook for 3 minutes more.

Fold the cream mixture into the crab mixture, mixing well. Stuff the crab backs with the mixture, or in the baking dish. Bake for 15 to 20 minutes, or until hot and lightly browned on top. Check for doneness after the first 15 minutes. Serve while hot with Creole rémoulade sauce.

Creole Rémoulade Sauce

Makes 1 1/4 cups

1 cup mayonnaise

1/4 cup buttermilk

1 tablespoon capers

1 teaspoon Magnolias blackening spice (page 22)

1 teaspoon horseradish

Whisk all the ingredients together. Store in an airtight container and refrigerate for up to 1 week.

Beer-Battered Catfish Fries and Pickled Okra Rémoulade

Serves 6 to 8

6 (6-ounce) catfish fillets

1 cup all-purpose flour

2 teaspoons fine sea salt

Freshly ground black pepper

3 eggs, separated

2 ^{1}/$_2$ tablespoons vegetable oil

1 cup dark beer, room temperature

Vegetable or canola oil for deep frying

Pickled okra rémoulade (recipe follows)

On a cutting board, slice the catfish into fingers the size of steak fries. Refrigerate until ready to use.

In a large bowl, mix together the flour and salt, adding pepper as desired. In another bowl, whisk together the egg yolks, oil and beer. Gradually pour the liquid mixture into the dry mixture, whisking until completely free of lumps. Cover the bowl with plastic wrap and refrigerate for at least 2 hours, or overnight.

Preheat the oven to 225 degrees F, and place a baking pan in the oven to keep the catfish warm after cooking.

Pour 2 inches of oil into a heavy-bottomed skillet and heat to 375 degrees F. Meanwhile, beat the egg whites until stiff and gently fold into the batter. Pat the catfish dry and submerge the pieces into the batter one at a time. Fry one piece, taste for seasoning, and add more seasoning if needed. Fry the catfish 6 pieces at a time, cooking for 3 to 4 minutes, until golden brown. Place in the warm oven until all pieces have been fried. Serve with pickled okra rémoulade.

Pickled Okra Rémoulade

Makes 2 ^{3}/$_4$ cups

^{1}/$_3$ cup buttermilk

1 tablespoon Sriracha sauce

Juice and zest of ^{1}/$_2$ lemon

Juice and zest of 1 lime

1 cup pickled okra (page 43), coarsely chopped

1 tablespoon pickled okra juice

2 cups mayonnaise

^{1}/$_2$ teaspoon freshly ground black pepper

Pinch of cayenne pepper

Coarse sea salt

In a food processor or blender, combine the buttermilk, Sriracha, lemon juice and zest, lime juice and zest, and okra; blend until smooth. Transfer to a mixing bowl and whisk in the okra juice, mayonnaise, black pepper, and cayenne, seasoning to taste with salt. Store in an airtight container and refrigerate until ready to use.

Cheese Straws

Makes 7 ¹/₂ dozen

When it comes to cheese straws, we have a variety of recipes that float around the bakeshop— from blue cheese and bacon, Pepper Jack for a spicy variation, or pimiento cheese with pork crackling dust, to more traditional recipes like this one. This particular recipe has been around since the early '90s. When making cheese straws, it works better to let the butter come to room temperature before starting. Use block cheese and grate it yourself while the cheese is cold. However, let it come to room temperature after grating—it will cream together quicker.

4 ounces sharp white cheddar, shredded

4 ounces sharp yellow cheddar, shredded

¹/₂ cup salted butter, room temperature

1 teaspoon Old Bay seasoning

1 cup all-purpose flour

1 egg, beaten

Benne seeds

In the bowl of a stand mixer fitted with a paddle, mix the two cheeses, butter and Old Bay seasoning until creamy. Add in the flour and mix until just incorporated. Remove the dough from the bowl and roll into two small balls. Cover the dough with plastic wrap and place in the refrigerator to chill until firm, about 1 ¹/₂ hours.

While the dough is chilling, line 2 baking trays with parchment paper and preheat the oven to 325 degrees F. Remove the dough from the refrigerator, place on a floured surface and pat out to ¹/₈ to ¹/₄ inch thick. Cut the dough into strips 3 to 4 inches long and 1 inch wide. You can also place the dough in a pastry bag with a star tip or cookie extruder and pipe onto a prepared baking sheet. Take your beaten egg and lightly coat the top of the straws with a brush, then sprinkle with benne seeds. Bake in the middle rack of the oven for 10 to 15 minutes, until golden brown. Make sure to rotate the trays to ensure even cooking. Remove from the trays and allow to cool.

Boiled Peanut Hummus

Makes 3 3/4 cups

2 cups boiled peanuts (recipe follows)

2 tablespoons Roasted Garlic Purée (page 18)

1/3 cup tahini

2 tablespoons freshly squeezed lemon juice

1/2 teaspoon ground cumin

2 cups reserved cooking liquid, divided

Coarse sea salt

Freshly ground black pepper

Pickled okra (recipe follows)

Hot pepper relish (recipe follows)

Crackers

In a food processor fitted with a metal blade, add the peanuts, garlic, tahini, lemon juice, cumin and 1/2 cup of the reserved liquid. Turn on the machine and process until smooth, adding reserved liquid as needed. Season with salt and pepper to taste. Serve with pickled okra, hot pepper relish, and crackers.

Boiled Peanuts

Makes 2 cups

2 cups shelled dried raw peanuts

2 gallons water, divided

1/4 cup coarse sea salt

In a bucket, soak the peanuts overnight in 1 gallon of water, making sure the nuts are completely covered with water. After soaking, strain the peanuts.

In a heavy-bottomed pot big enough to hold the peanuts and 1 gallon water, cook the nuts on a low boil until soft, about 3 hours. Keep an eye on the water level and add a little more as needed, enough to keep the nuts covered while cooking. When soft, drain the peanuts, reserving 2 cups of the liquid for making the hummus.

Pickled Okra

1 1/2 pounds fresh okra

3 cloves garlic

6 medium-sized hot chile peppers

3 sprigs fresh dill

3 teaspoons mustard seed

1 tablespoon black peppercorns

1 3/4 cup water

1 1/4 cups rice wine vinegar

1 1/4 cups apple cider vinegar

2 tablespoon coarse sea salt

Warm the jars and divide the okra, garlic, hot peppers, dill, mustard seeds and peppercorns among 3 jars. In a small saucepan over medium-high heat, combine the water, vinegars and salt. Bring to a rolling boil. Pour the hot brine water into the jars, making sure to leave about 1/4 inch headspace at the top. Cap the jars with lids and hand tighten. Seal in a hot-water bath for 5 minutes (see "Canning, Pickling and Putting Up" on page 14). Allow to cool, then refrigerate. Let sit for 4 to 6 weeks before using. If you plan to use the okra immediately, it should pickle for at least overnight in jars before serving.

Hot Pepper Relish

Ram's Horn peppers are grown locally on Johns Island by farmer and longtime friend Dan Kennerty. He brings us our peppers about every three days when they are in season. They deliver a mild spicy heat that will always bring you back for more.

2 dozen Ram's Horn peppers

1 tablespoon olive oil

1 cup rice wine vinegar

2 tablespoons honey

2 green bell peppers, seeded and diced

2 red bell peppers, seeded and diced

1 yellow onion, finely diced

1 tablespoon chopped fresh parsley

Pinch of coarse sea salt

Preheat the oven to 350 degrees F.

Coat the Ram's Horn peppers in the olive oil and place on a baking tray with sides. Roast for 10 to 12 minutes, or until the peppers are soft and the skin is charred. Remove the peppers from the oven, place them in a bowl and cover with plastic wrap. This helps the skin separate from the pepper flesh. When cooled, remove the peppers from the bowl. Peel, remove seeds and cut the stems off the peppers. In a food processor, blend the Ram's Horn peppers with the vinegar and honey until smooth. Place the puréed peppers back into the bowl and add the green and red bell peppers, onion, parsley and salt. Store in an airtight container and refrigerate for up to 2 weeks.

Carolina Crab Cakes with Southern Shrimp and Hominy Succotash and Tomato Butter

This is the appetizer version of our crab cakes, served on a bed of shrimp and hominy succotash. We like to use whatever fresh beans and peas the farmers have available on the day that we're cooking it, so feel free to use whatever is in season. The succotash also goes great with grilled fish. Make the cakes bigger and serve as an entrée if desired.

1 pound jumbo lump crabmeat

1/2 cup Duke's mayonnaise

1 tablespoon Worcestershire sauce

1/2 teaspoon Old Bay seasoning

1 tablespoon chopped basil

1 teaspoon lemon zest

1/4 cup panko bread crumbs, plus more for coating

1/4 cup canola oil, divided

Coarse sea salt and cracked black pepper

Southern shrimp and hominy succotash (recipe follows)

Tomato butter (recipe follows)

All crabmeat should be carefully picked through to remove any shell. Try to keep the lumps intact and drain off any excess water.

In a medium-sized bowl, combine the mayonnaise, Worcestershire sauce, Old Bay, basil and lemon zest. In a separate medium-sized bowl, add the crabmeat and $1/4$ cup panko bread crumbs. Gently fold in the mayonnaise mixture. Form into 12 crab cakes and lightly cover with the additional panko bread crumbs. Refrigerate for 30 minutes before cooking.

Heat $1/8$ cup canola oil in a heavy-bottomed skillet and sauté 6 crab cakes over medium-high heat for 3 minutes on each side, or until golden brown. Transfer to a warm plate. Wipe the pan clean, add the remaining canola oil to the pan and repeat the process. Divide the hot shrimp and hominy succotash among 6 plates. Place 2 warm crab cakes on top, drizzle with Tomato Butter and serve immediately.

Southern Shrimp and Hominy Succotash
Makes 9 cups

1 teaspoon olive oil

$1/2$ cup diced onion

$1/2$ cup finely diced red pepper

$1/4$ cup diced celery

1 teaspoon minced garlic

$1 1/2$ cups cooked beans and peas (see page 177)

$3/4$ cup canned hominy, rinsed

$1 1/2$ cups cooked fresh yellow corn

24 large shrimp, peeled, deveined, tails removed (save shells and heads for stock)

2 cups stemmed and julienned fresh spinach

$1/2$ cup heavy cream

1 cup shrimp stock (see page 12)

Coarse sea salt and freshly ground black pepper

In a heavy-bottomed pan over medium heat, add the olive oil and sauté the onion, red pepper, celery and garlic until the onion is translucent. Add the beans, hominy, and yellow corn and mix well. Add the shrimp, spinach, cream and shrimp stock. Simmer, reduce by one-third, stirring occasionally, until the shrimp are pink and begin to curl and the spinach is wilted. Season with sea salt and pepper to taste.

Tomato Butter
Makes 2 $1/2$ cups

1 tablespoon olive oil

3 shallots, minced

1 cup tomato juice

$1/4$ cup whipping cream

$3/4$ pound (3 sticks) unsalted butter, cut into small pieces

$1/2$ teaspoon salt

Pinch of white pepper

Warm the olive oil in a heavy-bottomed saucepot over medium-high heat. Sauté the shallots until translucent. Add the tomato juice and reduce until it becomes bubbly and thick. Add the cream and reduce until thickened, stirring often. Turn the heat down and, stirring constantly, add the butter a little bit at a time until all is incorporated. Remove from heat and hold in a warm area until ready to serve.

Fried Green Tomatoes with Caramelized Onion and White Cheddar Grits, Country Ham and Tomato Chutney

Serves 6

3 cups all-purpose flour, seasoned with salt and pepper

3 cups buttermilk

3 eggs

2 cups panko bread crumbs

3/4 cup yellow cornmeal

1/3 cup julienned fresh basil

18 (1/4-inch-thick) slices green tomatoes (about 5 whole tomatoes)

4 cups canola oil

Tomato chutney (recipe follows)

Caramelized onion and white cheddar grits (recipe follows)

Tomato butter (see page 45)

6 (1 1/2-ounce) slices country ham, halved

This is a standard breading procedure that can be used for frying many kinds of vegetables. You'll need 3 separate containers, or use 3 large freezer bags to save time on the cleanup. Place the seasoned flour in the first container or bag. In the second, mix the buttermilk and eggs together. In the third, mix the panko, cornmeal and basil. Evenly coat all tomatoes in the seasoned flour, shaking off the excess. Place in the buttermilk mixture, remove the tomatoes and shake off any excess. Place them in the final pan of panko-cornmeal mixture, making sure to coat them well. (As you work to coat the tomatoes, try to keep one hand dry and use your other hand for the wet steps.) In a large skillet or deep fryer, heat the canola oil to 325 degrees F. Fry the tomatoes in small batches until golden brown,

about 3 to 4 minutes. Place on a brown paper bag to drain and keep warm.

Choose any good country ham and allow 1 1/2 ounces or 2 pieces of thinly sliced ham per person.

Sear the ham in a sauté pan. Place 6 appetizer-sized plates on the counter. In the center of each plate, place a 3-ounce scoop of caramelized onion and white cheddar grits. Starting with a single slice of fried green tomato, top the grits with alternating slices of tomato and ham. Finish the stack with a slice of tomato. Crown the stack with a spoonful of the tomato chutney. Finish the dish using a 2-ounce ladle to drizzle the tomato butter around the outside of the plate.

Tomato Chutney

Serves 6

4 cups sugar

2 cups apple cider vinegar

6 cups julienned tomatoes, drained

2 cups julienned yellow onions

1 jalapeño, minced

2 teaspoons red pepper flakes

Place the sugar and vinegar in heavy-bottomed saucepot over medium-high heat and bring to a boil. Reduce the heat to a simmer and reduce the volume by half. Add the remaining ingredients and cook for about 1 hour, until the mixture becomes syrup-like. Remember that it will thicken as it cools. After it cooks down, remove from the heat and cool.

Caramelized Onion and White Cheddar Grits   *Serves 6*

3 cups water

1 cup stone-ground grits

$^1/_2$ cup heavy cream

1 small onion, julienned and caramelized

1 cup grated white cheddar cheese

Coarse sea salt and freshly ground black pepper

In a heavy-bottomed pot, bring the water to boil. Slowly stir in the grits and stir continuously for the first 5 minutes to prevent lumps. Turn the heat down to low and simmer for 30 minutes, stirring occasionally. Add the heavy cream and cook for 15 minutes more. The grits should be thick and plump; add more water or heavy cream if needed. Stir in the caramelized onion and white cheddar cheese. Cook for 5 minutes more. Season to taste with salt and pepper. Keep warm until ready to serve.

Fried Mac and Cheese with Red-eye Bacon Jam and Hot Pepper Relish

Serves 6 to 8

Marshall Tucker, aka Ms. Marshall, has been working with me for many years. The woman makes the best red rice, mac & cheese, and collard greens you've ever tasted. Truth be known, I think she walks around with a bag of secret spices in her pocket. I don't know the names of the secret spices, but whatever they are, the magic never fails in these signature recipes.

MS. MARSHALL'S MAC & CHEESE

1 $1/2$ gallons water

2 tablespoon salt

8 cups elbow macaroni

5 cups heavy cream

1 cup sour cream

$1/2$ cup prepared mustard

1 tablespoon butter

2 tablespoons sea salt

6 eggs, beaten

9 cups shredded yellow cheddar cheese, divided

TO FINISH

Canola oil for frying

2 cups all-purpose flour

Red-eye bacon jam (recipe follows)

Hot pepper relish (see page 43)

MS. MARSHALL'S MAC & CHEESE: Preheat the oven to 350 degrees F.

Bring the water to a boil in a large stock pot. Add the salt just before adding the macaroni and cook until al dente, about 12 minutes. Remember the noodles are going to be cooked again, so don't overcook them. Drain and rinse the elbows in cold water with a few ice cubes to quickly cool. Don't oil the noodles. Place the macaroni in a large bowl, cover loosely and set aside.

In another bowl, combine the heavy cream, sour cream, mustard, butter, salt, eggs and 6 cups cheddar cheese. Mix well and pour the mixture over the macaroni, making sure it's well coated. Pour into a large baking dish and cover with foil. Bake at 350 degrees F for 30 minutes. Pull the dish from the oven and remove the foil; sprinkle the remaining 3 cups cheddar cheese on top. Return to the oven uncovered and allow the cheese to brown just a little. Take out and enjoy immediately. If serving as a side, serves 10 to 12

family style. If using for the fried mac & cheese, this recipe will need to be chilled overnight.

TO FINISH: Using the chilled Ms. Marshall's mac & cheese, cut 24 bite-sized squares measuring about 1 $1/2$ x 1 $1/2$ inches each. Place on a sheet tray and put them in the freezer for about 30 minutes (do not freeze).

In a heavy skillet or deep fryer, heat 2 inches of oil to 350 degrees F. Dredge each square in flour and fry for about 60 seconds on each side, or until golden brown. Drain on a paper towel. Place 3 to 4 squares on each plate and top with the red-eye bacon jam. Spoon a little hot pepper relish on top and serve.

NOTE: If you don't have time to make and cool the mac & cheese in advance of frying, you can substitute any of my homemade pimiento cheese recipes if you have some on hand. Use about 2 ounces and follow the same method above for frying.

Red-eye Bacon Jam

Makes 2 ¼ cups

1 pound applewood-smoked bacon or bacon ends, chopped

1 yellow onion, minced

1 tablespoon minced garlic

1 (10-ounce) jar piquillo peppers, drained

¹/₂ cup freshly brewed coffee

¹/₂ cup good-quality maple syrup

¹/₄ cup firmly packed brown sugar

In a cast iron skillet, cook the bacon until crispy. Remove the skillet from heat and pour off all but 1 tablespoon of drippings. Be sure to save the reserved drippings for later use. Chop the bacon and set aside.

Place the skillet back on the heat and sauté the onion until translucent. Add the garlic and peppers, and sauté briefly, for 1 to 2 minutes. Stir in the coffee, syrup, brown sugar, and chopped bacon, and cook for 30 minutes over low heat. Remove the skillet from heat. Place the mixture in a food processor and pulse a few times. Do not liquefy. Chill and place in an airtight container until ready to use. Serve warm.

Pan-Seared Sea Scallops with Lowcountry Hoe Cakes, Spinach, Apple-Brandy Cream and Balsamic Vinegar Reduction

Serves 6

All the sauces can be made in advance, just be sure to warm them slowly. The hoe cake batter can made ahead of time too, but the scallops need to be cooked right before serving.

Salt and freshly ground black pepper

18 diver scallops (about 2 pounds)

$^1/_2$ tablespoon olive oil

Spinach (recipe follows, can be made ahead)

Hoe cakes (recipe follows, batter can be made ahead)

Apple-brandy cream sauce (recipe follows, can be made ahead)

Balsamic reduction (recipe follows, can be made ahead)

Dust the scallops with salt and pepper. Sauté scallops until medium, about 2 minutes per side. Place on a warm plate until ready to serve.

TO FINISH: Place the spinach in the center of a plate, top with 3 hoe cakes and place 1 scallop on top of each hoe cake. Spoon the apple-brandy cream sauce over the scallops. Using the back of a spoon, drizzle the balsamic reduction over the dish. Enjoy.

Spinach

Makes about 1 cup

$^1/_2$ tablespoon butter

1 $^1/_2$ pounds fresh spinach

Coarse sea salt and freshly ground black pepper

In a medium-sized skillet, add the butter and sauté the spinach until wilted. Season to taste with salt and pepper. Remove from heat and keep warm. Spinach wilts to about 1 cup after cooking.

Hoe Cakes

Makes 18 cakes

1 1/2 cups yellow cornmeal

2 1/2 cups all-purpose flour

3 tablespoons brown sugar

1 tablespoon salt

1 tablespoon ground cumin

Pinch of cayenne pepper

Pinch of freshly ground black pepper

4 eggs, beaten

2 cups whole milk

1 cup heavy cream

1 onion, diced

1 cup corn from freshly shucked cob

In a small mixing bowl, combine the cornmeal, flour, brown sugar, salt, cumin, cayenne, and black pepper and set aside. In a blender, add eggs, milk, heavy cream, onion, and sweet corn and purée well. Add the puréed mixture to the dry ingredients and mix well. Set aside.

Cook the hoe cake batter as you would silver dollar pancakes, allowing 3 pancakes per person. Keep the cakes warm until ready to serve.

Apple-Brandy Cream Sauce

Makes about 1 cup

1 shallot, finely diced

10 pieces applewood-smoked bacon, chopped and cooked

1 Granny Smith apple, diced

1/2 cup brandy

3 cups heavy cream

1 tablespoon chopped fresh parsley

Salt and freshly ground black pepper

In a medium-sized sauté pan, sauté the shallot and bacon until bacon is rendered. Add the apples and cook until soft. Deglaze the pan with brandy and burn off the alcohol. Add the cream and reduce by two-thirds. Add the parsley, season with salt and pepper and keep warm.

Balsamic Reduction

Makes 12 ounces

1 pint balsamic vinegar

1 cup port wine

In a small saucepot over medium-high heat, add the balsamic vinegar and port wine. Reduce the liquid until it reaches the consistency of syrup.

Tomato Pie

Makes one 9-inch pie

July and August mean big, juicy, vine-ripened tomatoes, outdoor parties, barbecues and unexpected friends who show up on my doorstep ready for a little beach time. It's the season of big, fat watermelons, sweet corn and all the bounty of summer just bursting with flavor. This recipe for tomato pie is a great way to capture the essence of it all. You can use any variety of sun-ripened tomatoes. If you enjoy your pie a little more juicy than firm, don't salt or drain the tomatoes.

If you're in a hurry and don't have time to make the crust, take the simple route and crack open a can of crescent rolls, roll them all together and flatten into a simple crust. Turns out great every time. Buying a premade crust works well, too.

3–4 tomatoes (about 2 pounds), peeled and sliced

1 1/4 teaspoon sea salt, divided

1 (9-inch) pie crust (recipe follows)

3 green onions, thinly sliced

6 leaves fresh basil, chopped

1/2 teaspoon freshly ground black pepper

1 cup mayonnaise

2 cups shredded yellow cheddar cheese

In a colander, arrange the tomatoes in a single layer and sprinkle with 1/4 teaspoon salt. Allow to drain for about 20 minutes. Pat dry the tomatoes.

Preheat the oven to 350 degrees F. In the pie crust, layer the tomatoes, green onions and basil, seasoning each layer with the remaining salt and the pepper. In a medium-size bowl, stir together the mayonnaise and cheese. Spread the mixture over the top of the pie, and bake for 30 minutes. Serve warm or at room temperature.

Savory Pie Crust

Makes two (9-inch) pie crusts

1 cup White Lily Self-Rising flour

3/4 cup yellow cornmeal

3/4 teaspoon sea salt

1 stick (1/2 cup) unsalted butter, cut into cubes and kept cold

6 tablespoons grated Parmesan cheese, divided

4–5 tablespoons cold water

In a food processor fitted with a metal blade, pulse the flour, cornmeal, and salt until

combined. Add the butter and 3 tablespoons Parmesan; pulse the mixture until it looks like coarse meal dotted with small bits of butter. Slowly add 4 tablespoons water, one at a time. Pulse until the dough comes together. If needed, add 1 more tablespoon cold water. Wrap the crust in plastic wrap and refrigerate for 30 minutes.

Divide the dough in half and roll each half out on a floured surface to around 13 inches for 9-inch pie pans. (You may reserve the other half of dough for later use by wrapping in plastic wrap and freezing.) Place the dough into a 9-inch pie plate, pressing the dough evenly into the bottom and sides of the plate. Use a fork to pierce holes in the bottom of the crust. Chill in the refrigerator until firm. Preheat the oven to 350 degrees F.

Remove the crust from the refrigerator. To blind bake, cover the crust with foil and top with dried beans. (This will prevent the crust from rising too much.) Bake the crust for about 20 minutes. Remove the beans and foil and bake for another 5 minutes, until the crust is golden brown. Transfer to a wire rack and sprinkle the bottom with the remaining 3 tablespoons Parmesan while still warm, then chill.

All over the South, pimiento cheese dips are long-standing favorites. Every family has their own recipes, some handed down from generation to generation. Some use sharp white cheddar, some use yellow cheddar and some call for Parmesan, while others use cream cheese or a spunky Pepper Jack. Creative combinations incorporate everything from nuts and spicy peppers to olives of all kinds. Some families will use nothing less than Duke's mayonnaise, while others claim that nothing will do but Hellmann's, and some even use Miracle Whip. My mom chose Miracle Whip, but we'll keep that a secret. The pimiento cheese dip recipes I've included in this book are versions of some of the best in the South that I've ever tasted.

Pawley's Island Pimiento Cheese   *Makes 8 cups*

This one is from a friend up in Pawley's Island, South Carolina. We had dinner at his home some years ago, and this is the cheese spread he served.

5 cups grated sharp yellow cheddar cheese

8 ounces cream cheese, room temperature

1 cup grated Parmesan cheese

1 teaspoon finely grated onion

3/4 cup Duke's mayonnaise

1 large red bell pepper, roasted, peeled, seeded and diced, or 1 (8-ounce) jar whole peeled pimientos, drained, rinsed and diced

1 teaspoon cayenne pepper or ground red pepper

Cracked black pepper

Flatbread or crackers

In the bowl of a stand mixer, beat the cheddar cheese, Parmesan cheese, cream cheese, onion and mayo for 1 to 2 minutes, then add the bell pepper or pimientos, cayenne and black pepper. Mix until not quite smooth. Serve it with flatbread or your choice of crackers.

Charleston Caviar

Makes 8 cups

This is another favorite of mine. It's a version from a friend's mom who also lives in Charleston.

1 1/4 pounds sharp white cheddar cheese, shredded

1/4 cup grated Parmesan cheese

1 cup chopped pimiento-stuffed green olives

1/4 cup Hellmann's mayonnaise

1 tablespoon chopped fresh parsley

1/2 teaspoon freshly ground black pepper

2 1/2 cups jarred red pimientos, drained, rinsed and diced, or 5 red bell peppers, roasted, peeled, seeded and chopped

Dash of ground red pepper

In a mixing bowl, combine all of the ingredients except the ground red pepper, and mix well. Season to taste with ground red pepper. Store in the refrigerator until ready to use.

Mr. Brown's Pimiento Cheese

Makes 5 cups

This was the first pimiento cheese recipe I tried with bacon in it. I was a guest chef for a Meals on Wheels charity in Wilmington, Delaware, called Meals for the Masters. This recipe is also great to use on top of burgers and steaks.

1/2 cup cooked and chopped applewood-smoked bacon

1/4 cup Duke's mayonnaise

1/2 cup mascarpone cheese

1 cup shredded sharp white cheddar cheese

1/4 cup shredded Parmesan cheese

1 tablespoon minced jalapeño pepper

1/4 cup chopped jarred piquillo peppers

1 1/2 teaspoons smoked paprika

2 tablespoons chopped flat-leaf parsley

Salt and freshly ground black pepper to taste

In the bowl of a stand mixer fitted with a paddle, mix all of the ingredients until the peppers are well incorporated. Refrigerate until ready to use.

Isle of Palms Pimiento Cheese

Makes 4 cups

This one is from my dear friend Fry Daddy. He has a great theory on walking home later in the evening from your favorite cold-beer stop on the beach: You know you're going the right way if you keep your right foot wet. That is, if you live north. I am not sure why a few people in the Charleston area are called "Daddy-something," but three of my friends have this distinguished moniker: Fry Daddy, aka John Fry; Fish Daddy, aka Leo; and Daddy Rabbit, aka Harold Timmerman, the oldest of the group at 75. Maybe it's the wisdom of elders growing up on the water over at the beach. Now here it is, Fry Daddy's recipe.

2 cups shredded sharp white cheddar cheese

8 ounces cream cheese

1/2 cup Duke's mayonnaise

1/4 teaspoon cayenne pepper

1 jalapeño pepper, seeded and finely minced (add the seeds if you want more heat)

1 red bell pepper, roasted, peeled, seeded and diced, or 1 (4-ounce) jar whole peeled pimientos, drained, rinsed and diced

1 teaspoon diced onion

Sea salt and freshly ground black pepper

In the bowl of a stand mixer, place the cheddar cheese, cream cheese, mayonnaise, cayenne, jalapeño, bell pepper or pimiento, and diced onion. Beat at a medium speed until well combined. Check for seasoning and add salt and pepper as needed. Place in the refrigerator until ready to use.

Cypress Pimiento Cheese

Makes 3 cups

This next recipe is from Craig Deihl, the executive chef of both Cypress and Artisan Meat Share in Charleston.

1 cup shredded sharp yellow cheddar cheese

1/2 cup mascarpone cheese

1/4 cup jarred piquillo peppers, puréed

1/4 cup Duke's mayonnaise

1 1/2 teaspoon smoked hot paprika

1 teaspoon white pepper

1/4 cup shredded Parmesan cheese

2 tablespoons chopped flat-leaf parsley

Salt and freshly ground black pepper

In a medium-sized mixing bowl, combine all the ingredients, season with salt and pepper to taste, and incorporate evenly.

Shrimp Paste

$1/2$ cup plus 2 tablespoons butter, cool room temperature

$1 1/2$ pounds shrimp, peeled and deveined

$1/4$ cup minced onion

2 tablespoons sherry

3 tablespoons lemon juice

1 teaspoon prepared horseradish

$2/3$ cup Duke's mayonnaise

$1/2$ teaspoon coarse sea salt

$1/4$ teaspoon white pepper

In a large skillet, melt 2 tablespoons of butter. Add the shrimp and sauté until pink and cooked through. Remove shrimp from the pan and set aside. Add the onion and sauté briefly, about 1 minute, then deglaze the pan with sherry. Remove from heat.

Using a food processor fitted with a metal blade, add the shrimp and pulse until chopped. Add the liquid from the pan add the lemon juice, horse-radish, mayonnaise, remaining $1/2$ cup butter, salt and pepper. Mix until smooth. Transfer to a buttered bowl or ramekin and chill in the refrigerator.

To unmold, run a knife around the bowl and the paste should slide right out. Serve with toast points, little biscuits or crackers.

SALADS & DRESSINGS

Tomato, Cucumber and Black-Eyed Pea Salad

Serves 8 to 10

This is a great summer salad when tomatoes, cucumbers and peas are at the farmers market. Choose heirloom or cherry tomatoes, like Green Cherokee, Sunburst or Chocolate Cherries. Grab a bag of peas and some herbs and lettuces. My favorites include arugula, red and green oak leaf, Romaine, baby Boston, frisée, and cress—a combination of peppery and sweet lettuce mix.

4 cups cooked fresh black-eyed peas, or 2 (15-ounce) cans, drained

$1/2$ cup sherry vinegar

2 tablespoons honey

$1/4$ cup olive oil

1 clove garlic, crushed and minced

1 jalapeño, seeded and minced

2 tablespoons chopped fresh parsley

2 teaspoons chopped fresh marjoram leaves

1 teaspoon cumin seeds, toasted and finely ground

1 green bell pepper, seeded and diced

1 red bell pepper, seeded and diced

1 cucumber, peeled, seeded and cut into $1/4$-inch-thick slices

$1 1/2$ pounds mixed lettuces, washed and spun dry

Juice of 1 lemon

Coarse sea salt and cracked pepper

3 heirloom tomatoes, thickly sliced

$1 1/2$ cups crumbled feta cheese

4 slices cooked bacon, crumbled (optional)

If you are using fresh or dried beans, get them started. When cooked, let them cool and set aside.

In a small bowl, combine the sherry vinegar, honey, olive oil, garlic, jalapeño, parsley, marjoram and cumin. Mix well and set aside.

In a medium-sized bowl, combine the cooled black-eyed peas, bell peppers and cucumbers. Pour in the vinegar mixture and toss well. Check for seasoning. Chill in the refrigerator for 2 hours or overnight.

In a large bowl, toss the salad with the lemon juice and add salt and pepper as desired. Place 2 tomato slices on each plate. Equally divide the lettuces among the plates, and place $1/2$ cup of the marinated black-eyed pea mixture on top of the lettuces. Sprinkle with crumbled feta cheese and bacon.

ᐧ{ KEEPING LETTUCE CRISP }ᐧ

A lot of times lettuces really get hit hard by the heat, so here's a helpful hint: When you wash the lettuces, add a few cups of ice to the water and let them sit for about 10 minutes to crisp them up and bring them back to life. Be sure to use a salad spinner to eliminate as much water from the greens as possible before tossing them in the salad.

Broccoli and Pistachio Salad

Serves 6 to 8

4 cups finely chopped broccoli florets

1 cup minced peeled broccoli stems

1 cup mayonnaise

4 tablespoons whole grain mustard

$1/2$ cup dried cranberries

$1/2$ cup shelled pistachios

2 tablespoons sugar

2 tablespoons celery salt

1 tablespoon cider vinegar

1 tablespoon finely grated fresh ginger

1 tablespoon orange zest

1 teaspoon freshly ground black pepper

Juice of 1 lemon

Combine all of the ingredients and adjust seasoning if necessary. Refrigerate for 1 hour before serving.

BBQ Chicken Salad

Serves 6

This is our version of a southern cobb salad. Feel free to use chicken or leftover pulled pork. Use any beans that you have on hand; canned beans work just as well as slow-cooked beans in this recipe.

1 1/2 pounds chicken tenders

1 cup South Carolina mustard sauce (see page 24) or store-bought barbecue sauce

2 heads Romaine lettuce, chopped, or 16 cups salad mix, washed and spun dry

Spicy buttermilk ranch dressing (recipe follows) or store-bought spicy ranch dressing

6 hard-boiled eggs, peeled and chopped

1 large tomato, diced

2 avocados, diced

Cornbread croutons (see page 32)

1 cup cooked red beans, drained and rinsed

1 cup grilled sweet corn relish (see page 13)

6 strips bacon, cooked and crumbled

1 1/2 cups shredded Pepper Jack cheese

Preheat the oven to 350 degrees F. Grill or fry the chicken tenders and toss them with the barbecue sauce. Place in the oven to keep warm.

Use a large salad bowl or 6 separate bowls. Pile in the Romaine or salad mix and give it a light coating of the ranch dressing. Top the lettuce with the remaining ingredients in thin rows of the following order: chopped eggs, tomato, avocados, cornbread croutons, cooked chicken, red beans, corn relish, bacon and shredded cheese. Serve with additional ranch dressing on the side.

Spicy Buttermilk Ranch Dressing

Makes 4 cups (32 ounces)

2 tablespoons sugar

1/4 cup (2 ounces) apple cider vinegar

3 cups Duke's mayonnaise

1 cup (8 ounces) buttermilk

1/2 tablespoon smoked paprika

1/2 tablespoon sea salt

1 tablespoon chopped fresh dill

1 tablespoon chopped fresh thyme

1 tablespoon garlic powder

1/2 tablespoon onion powder

1 teaspoon white pepper

In a small bowl, dissolve the sugar in the apple cider vinegar. Place all of the ingredients in a blender. Blend well. Store in a Mason jar in the refrigerator.

Rocket Lettuce with Poached Pear, Blue Cheese, Candied Pecans and Lingonberry Vinaigrette

Serves 6

Pears are one of my favorite fruits to eat, and this is a great salad to make when they come into season. Blue cheese is another favorite of mine. From smoked blue cheese on grilled steaks to melted blue on potato chips, I love it on almost everything. If you can't find Clemson blue cheese where you live, substitute another blue cheese of good quality. The best and quickest way to make the lingonberry vinaigrette is in a blender.

1 1/2 pounds arugula, washed and spun dry

1 cup lingonberry vinaigrette (recipe follows), divided

6 whole poached pears (recipe follows)

1 1/2 cups Clemson blue cheese

1 1/2 cups candied pecans (see page 77)

In a large bowl, toss the arugula with 3/4 cup vinaigrette.

Place 6 plates on the counter. To assemble the salad, place a whole pear in the middle of each plate. Equally divide the arugula among the plates, placing beside each pear. Take a small ladle and drizzle some of the remaining vinaigrette around each pear and lettuce mound. Sprinkle 1/4 cup blue cheese on each salad, followed by 1/4 cup pecans.

Poached Pears

6 pears

1 gallon water

2 cups sugar

1 lemon, halved and juiced

1 cinnamon stick

1 vanilla bean, split

Peel the pears, leaving the stems on. In a medium to large pot, add water, sugar, lemon halves, cinnamon stick and vanilla bean. Place the pears in the cold liquid. Simmer the pears on medium heat (do not boil) until tender, about 20 minutes. Cool the pears and their poaching liquid in an ice bath. When cool, use a melon baller to scoop out the seeds. Place the pears in a container and cover with the chilled poaching liquid until ready to serve.

Lingonberry Vinaigrette

Makes 2 1/2 cups (20 ounces)

3 tablespoons Champagne vinegar

1/4 cup (2 ounces) freshly squeezed lemon juice

2 tablespoons Dijon mustard

1 cup (8 ounces) canola oil

1/3 cup lingonberry preserves

2 tablespoons finely julienned fresh basil leaves

2 tablespoons minced fresh parsley

2 tablespoons minced fresh chives

1/4 teaspoon freshly ground black pepper

1/2 teaspoon minced garlic

In a blender, combine the vinegar, lemon juice, and mustard and process at a low speed. Slowly stream in the canola oil until well emulsified. Add the lingonberry preserves and process for about 10 seconds. Pour into a Mason jar or bowl, and add the basil, parsley, chives, pepper and garlic. Shake well or whisk. Will keep for 1 week refrigerated.

Grilled Salmon BLT Salad

Serves 6

The Lemon-Caper Vinaigrette has a summer flair with the addition of sweet Vidalia onion. I also like to substitute or add things like tomatoes, avocados and a variety of seasonal fresh herbs or fruits.

6 (4–5 ounce) salmon fillets

3 tablespoons olive oil, divided

Coarse sea salt and cracked black pepper

6 (1/2-inch-thick) slices ciabatta bread or French baguette

12 pieces cooked applewood-smoked bacon

2 teaspoons roasted garlic purée (see page 18)

1 (3/4-pound) log goat cheese, sliced into 6 rounds

3/4 pound arugula, washed and spun dry

3/4 cup lemon caper vinaigrette (recipe follows)

3 large beefsteak tomatoes, each cut into 4 slices

1/2 small red onion, julienned

In a medium-sized bowl, lightly coat the salmon fillets with 1 tablespoon olive oil and season with salt and pepper.

Brush the bread with the remaining 2 tablespoons olive oil and sprinkle with salt and pepper.

Preheat the grill to 350 degrees, or use a large skillet over medium heat and cook the bacon until crispy. Remove the bacon from the pan; pour off the drippings and save for later use. Place the brushed ciabatta into the pan or onto the grill and toast both sides. Top each slice with roasted garlic purée and a slice of goat cheese and remove from the pan or grill. Keep warm.

In the same pan, sear the salmon on both sides for about 3 minutes. Remove from the heat and keep warm. (If using a grill, place the fillets at an angle towards 2 o'clock; in 2 minutes rotate them to 9 o'clock. Turn the fillets over and repeat the same rotating process. This process helps create nice grill marks on the fish at time of service.)

In a medium-sized bowl, lightly toss the arugula with 1/3 cup vinaigrette.

Place 6 plates on the counter. Place 1 roasted garlic and goat cheese crouton in the middle of each plate. Then crisscross 2 slices of bacon on top of each slice of bread. Place a small handful of arugula, a tomato slice, more arugula, another tomato, then more arugula. Top with the fish. When you plate the fish, place the good side down first and present it that way. (The good side is the flesh closest to the bone.) We use a decorative sweetgrass toothpick to hold it in place. Finish each stack with a pinch of red onion on top. Use a small spoon to drizzle the remaining vinaigrette around the outside of the plate for garnish.

Lemon-Caper Vinaigrette

Makes 4 cups (32 ounces)

1/4 cup finely diced Vidalia onion

1 cup (8 ounces) freshly squeezed lemon juice

1/4 cup (2 ounces) honey

2 tablespoons Dijon mustard

1 cup (8 ounces) extra virgin olive oil

1 cup (8 ounces) canola oil

1/4 cup capers

1 cup peeled, seeded and diced tomatoes

1/4 cup finely diced red bell pepper (about 1/2 pepper)

1/4 cup minced fresh chives*

1 tablespoon sea salt

1 tablespoon freshly ground black pepper

Place the onion and lemon juice in a bowl and let sit for about 10 minutes.

Add the honey and Dijon mustard. Slowly add the olive oil and canola oil, steadily whisking to combine. Add the capers, tomatoes, bell pepper and chives. Place in a Mason jar and give it a couple of good shakes before you use it. Will keep for 1 week refrigerated.

If you don't plan on using the vinaigrette right away, add the minced chives right before serving to retain their color.

Johns Island–Asparagus Salad with Deviled Eggs, Pancetta, Arugula and Pine Nuts

Serves 6

This green goddess dressing is a best effort at making this classic dressing from the famous Palace Hotel. I decided not to add garlic to my recipe. According to legend, you're supposed to rub the garlic along the inside of the salad bowl and hand tear the lettuce.

1/3 pound pancetta, diced

2 tablespoons butter

2 bunches asparagus spears, cut diagonally into 3/4-inch pieces

3/4 cup thinly sliced leeks, white and green parts

6 deviled eggs (recipe follows)

1 1/2 pounds arugula, washed and spun dry

1 cup 8 ounces green goddess dressing (recipe follows)

1/3 cup pine nuts

Coarse sea salt and pepper

In a large skillet over medium-high heat, sauté the pancetta until crispy. Remove from the pan and keep warm. Add the butter to the same pan, along with the asparagus and leeks. Sauté the asparagus and leeks until tender, 2 to 3 minutes. Remove from heat and keep warm.

Place 6 large salad bowls on the counter. At the base of the plate evenly divide the leeks. Place the asparagus spears crisscrossing like a herringbone necklace in the center of the plate. Place 1 deviled egg on each side of the plate.

In a large bowl, add the arugula and dressing and toss lightly. Equally divide the arugula among the plates and place on top of the asparagus. Garnish with the pancetta and pine nuts.

Deviled Eggs

Makes 12 deviled eggs

6 eggs

3 tablespoons Duke's mayonnaise

2 tablespoons sweet pickle relish

1 teaspoon prepared mustard

Pinch of salt

Place the eggs in a medium-sized saucepot, cover with cold water and bring to a boil. Cover, remove from heat and let sit for 12 minutes. Drain the water, and then shake the eggs back and forth in the drained pan to start cracking the shells. Peel under cold running water and set aside.

Cut the eggs in half and carefully remove the egg yolks. Place the yolks in a small bowl and mash with a fork, stirring in the remaining ingredients. Using a spoon or piping bag, fill the egg whites with the mixture. Place on a large plate and chill until ready to serve.

Green Goddess Dressing

2 teaspoons anchovy paste, or 3–4 oil-packed anchovies, rinsed and chopped

$^1/_2$ Hass avocado, peeled

$^3/_4$ cup mayonnaise

$^1/_3$ cup sour cream or crème fraîche

$^1/_3$ cup buttermilk

$^1/_2$ cup chopped fresh flat-leaf parsley

$^1/_4$ cup chopped fresh tarragon

3 tablespoons chopped fresh chives

2 tablespoons freshly squeezed lemon juice

1 tablespoon tarragon vinegar

Coarse sea salt and freshly ground black pepper

Place all of the ingredients in a food processor or blender and process for about 10 seconds, until smooth and green. Taste and adjust seasoning as needed. Thin with a little water if needed. Will keep for 1 week refrigerated.

Herb-Grilled Chicken Salad

Serves 6

This salad is made with locally harvested lettuces, feta cheese, cornbread croutons, sweet corn relish, beefsteak tomatoes and a honey-chipotle vinaigrette. To save time, you can buy canned chipotle paste rather than making your own.

2 tablespoons olive oil

1 1/2 tablespoons soy sauce

1 tablespoon chopped fresh oregano, or 2 teaspoons dried

1 tablespoon chopped fresh thyme, or 2 teaspoons dried

1 tablespoon chopped fresh basil, or 2 teaspoons dried

1/2 teaspoon onion powder

1/2 teaspoon granulated garlic

1/2 teaspoon freshly ground black pepper

1 1/2 pounds boneless chicken breasts (about 4 ounces each)

1 1/2 pounds mixed lettuces, washed and spun dry

1 1/2 cups honey-chipotle vinaigrette (recipe follows)

3 beefsteak tomatoes, each cut into 6 wedges

3 cups grilled sweet corn relish (see page 13)

24 cornbread croutons (see page 32)

1 1/2 cups crumbled feta cheese

In a medium-sized bowl, combine olive oil, soy sauce, oregano, thyme, basil, onion powder, garlic and pepper. Mix well. Toss the chicken breast with the marinade, cover, and place in the refrigerator for 3 to 4 hours or overnight.

Fire up the grill to 350 degrees F. Place the marinated chicken breast on the hot grill at an angle towards 2 o'clock. Close the grill and cook for 3 minutes. Rotate the chicken to a 9 o'clock position and cook for 2 minutes more. Turn the chicken over and repeat the rotations. Remove the chicken from the grill and let rest before slicing.

Place 6 full-sized plates on the counter. To serve the salad, toss the lettuces lightly with the vinaigrette. Mound about 2 cups lettuce per plate. Top each with chicken slices and place 3 tomato quarters on each plate at 2, 6 and 10 o'clock positions. Spoon 1/2 cup Corn Relish onto each one, add 4 Cornbread Croutons and sprinkle with feta cheese.

Honey-Chipotle Vinaigrette

Makes 4 cups (32 ounces)

3/4 cup (6 ounces) honey

2 tablespoons Creole mustard

1 tablespoon prepared horseradish

3 pieces pickled okra (see page 43, optional)

1 tablespoon chipotle paste (see page 99)

1/4 cup (2 ounces) orange juice

1 1/2 cups (12 ounces) apple cider vinegar

2 teaspoons coarse sea salt

2 cups (16 ounces) canola oil

In a blender combine all of the ingredients except the canola oil. Once blended, slowly add the oil until well incorporated. Pour into a Mason jar and refrigerate until ready to use.

SOUPS

Grilled Vidalia Onion Soup with Pepper Jack Cheese, Jalapeño Cornbread and Crispy Onion Straws

Serves 4 to 5

6 Vidalia onions, halved

3 red onions, halved

2 tablespoons olive oil

1/3 cup roasted garlic purée (see page 18)

6 cups chicken stock (see page 10)

1 1/2 teaspoons chili powder

1 tablespoon brown sugar

1/4 cup Sweet Baby Ray's barbecue sauce

1 bunch green onions, chopped

Coarse sea salt and freshly ground black pepper

4–5 slices jalapeño cornbread croutons (see page 32)

2 cups grated Pepper Jack cheese,

Fried onion straws (recipe follows)

12 chive stems, cut into 2-inch pieces

Begin by heating up the Weber grill or smoker to 250 to 300 degrees F. Grill or smoke the onions until tender. When done, remove and julienne the onions. In a heavy-bottomed pot over medium-high heat, add the olive oil and the julienned onions. Caramelize the onions to a dark mahogany color. Add garlic purée and cook for 2 minutes more. Add the chicken stock, chili powder, brown sugar, and barbecue sauce and bring the heat to a simmer. Reduce by one-third. In a blender, process the mixture until smooth. Add the green onions and check for seasoning, adding salt and pepper as desired. Remove the soup from heat and keep warm.

Preheat the broiler or preheat the oven to 500 degrees.

Ladle the soup into ovenproof bowls and place a cornbread crouton on top. Top each crouton with 1 slice of cheese, and brown under the broiler or in the oven until the cheese melts. Remove the bowls from the oven and top with the onion straws and chives.

Fried Onion Straws

Serves 5

Oil, enough to fill skillet 1 inch up the side

1 Vidalia onion, julienned

1/4 cup buttermilk

1/3 cup all-purpose flour

Pinch of coarse sea salt and freshly ground black pepper

In a medium skillet, heat the oil to 350 degrees F. Pour the buttermilk into a sandwich bag. Pour the flour into another and season with the salt and pepper. Coat the onion in the buttermilk. Remove the onion and shake off excess buttermilk. Add the onions to the flour and shake until coated. Remove and shake off the excess flour. Fry the onion straws in hot oil until crispy, about 2 minutes.

Heirloom Tomato Gazpacho with Bacon and Herb Croutons

Serves 6 to 8

Freeze any leftover soup in ice trays for Bloody Marys.

2 English cucumbers, halved lengthwise and seeded

2 red bell peppers, seeded

2 yellow bell peppers, seeded

4 heirloom Beefsteak tomatoes, cored, seeded and halved

2 red onions or sweet onions

5 cloves garlic, minced

6 cups (48 ounces) tomato juice

$1/2$ cup (4 ounces) sherry vinegar

$1/2$ cup extra virgin olive oil

1 tablespoon coarse sea salt

Freshly ground black pepper

Bacon-herb croutons (recipe follows)

$1/2$ cup (4 ounces) red wine vinegar

Coarsely chop all the vegetables. In a food processor fitted with a metal blade, purée half of the vegetables until smooth. Add the remaining half to the puréed mixture in the food processor and just pulse, leaving the vegetables a little chunky. Place the blended mixture in a large bowl. Add the garlic, tomato juice, sherry vinegar, olive oil, and salt. Gently combine and add pepper to taste. Chill the soup and let it sit for 4 hours before serving. Garnish with the croutons and red wine vinegar.

Bacon and Herb Croutons

Makes 5 cups

$1/4$ cup bacon drippings or olive oil

1 clove garlic, minced

2 tablespoons hot sauce

5 slices day-old bread, cut into cubes

$1/4$ cup grated Parmesan cheese

1 tablespoon chopped fresh basil

1 teaspoon chopped fresh cilantro

Preheat oven to 425 degrees F.

In a cast iron skillet over low heat, warm the bacon fat or olive oil and add the minced garlic, hot sauce and bread. Toss to coat the bread, and put the skillet in the oven for about 5 minutes, or until the croutons are light brown. Remove the skillet from the oven and place the croutons in a small bowl with the Parmesan, basil and cilantro. Toss well.

Sweet Potato and Butternut Squash Bisque with Spiced Cream and Candied Pecans

Serves 6 to 8

2 large butternut squash, peeled and cubed

2 sweet potatoes, peeled and cubed

3 tablespoons olive oil

2 tablespoons coarse sea salt, plus more for seasoning

2 tablespoons freshly ground black pepper, plus more for seasoning

4 tablespoons unsalted butter

1 large yellow onion, diced

2 carrots, peeled and diced

1 Granny Smith apple, peeled and diced

1 clove garlic, minced

10 cups chicken stock (see page 10)

1 teaspoon ground cinnamon

Pinch of nutmeg

2 cups heavy cream

Spiced whipped cream (recipe follows)

$^{1}/_{4}$ cup candied pecans (recipe follows)

Preheat the oven to 375 degrees F.

In a mixing bowl, coat the cubed squash and sweet potatoes with the olive oil, salt and pepper. Place the squash and potatoes on a baking sheet and roast for about 35 minutes, or until soft. Remove from the oven and set aside.

In a large, heavy-bottomed pan over medium-high heat, add the butter, onions and carrots; sauté until the onions are translucent and the carrots are soft. Add the apple and garlic and continue cooking for another 5 minutes. Add the chicken stock and the roasted vegetables. Bring to a boil, reduce to a simmer and cook for 15 minutes.

In a blender, purée the vegetables and stock in small batches. Pour the purée back into the pan and add cinnamon, nutmeg and heavy cream; season with salt and pepper to taste. Bring the soup back to a low simmer.

To serve, place a ladle of soup into each bowl and garnish with spiced whipped cream and candied pecans.

Spiced Whipped Cream

Makes 1 cup

1 cup heavy cream

$^1/_2$ teaspoon orange zest

Pinch of cinnamon

1 tablespoon honey

In a mixing bowl, whip the heavy cream, orange zest, cinnamon and honey until fluffy.

Candied Pecans

Makes 1 pound

This recipe calls for pecans, but you can substitute any kind of nut. Likewise, you can substitute vanilla or bourbon in place of water, or use honey instead of sugar.

1 cup sugar

$^1/_2$ teaspoon cayenne pepper

1 teaspoon cinnamon

$^1/_2$ teaspoon salt

2 egg whites

2 tablespoons water

1 pound pecan halves

Preheat the oven to 250 degrees F and line a sheet tray with parchment paper.

In a medium-sized bowl, combine the sugar, cayenne, cinnamon and salt; set aside.

Whisk together the egg whites and water. Add the pecans to the egg whites. Using a slotted spoon, mix the nuts until well coated. Slowly add the sugar mixture to the pecans and egg whites, making sure the nuts are well coated. Remove the nuts from the egg whites with the slotted spoon. Place the nuts on the parchment-lined sheet tray. Bake for 30 minutes, stirring about every 10 minutes, until medium golden brown. Store in an airtight container.

Chicken Soup with Tortillas and Lime

Serves 6 to 8

My lovely wife, Martha, makes this soup in the slow cooker after she roasts and pulls the chicken the night before. (If you make your chicken ahead, save the bones for the stock.) We used to be able to get away with one bird, but when the boys are home, we always need two. This soup goes fast.

2 tablespoons olive oil

1 yellow onion, diced

2 cloves garlic, minced

3 plum tomatoes, peeled and chopped

1 Pasilla chile pepper, roasted, seeded, peeled and chopped, or 1 (4-ounce) can diced green chiles

1 teaspoon ground cumin

1 dried bay leaf

1 teaspoon chili powder

1/4 cup cilantro leaves, chopped

1 1/4 cups enchilada sauce (recipe follows) or store-bought

1 1/2 pounds chicken, cooked and shredded

3 cups spicy black beans (see page 175), or 2 (14-ounce) cans black beans

4 cups chicken stock (see page 10)

Coarse sea salt and freshly ground black pepper

10 corn tortillas

2 limes, cut into wedges

1 Hass avocado, sliced

In a medium-sized saucepot over medium heat, add the olive oil and sauté the onion and garlic until the onion is translucent. Add the tomatoes, Pasilla pepper or green chiles, cumin, bay leaf, chili powder, cilantro, and enchilada sauce. Cook for 5 minutes and add the shredded chicken, black beans and chicken stock. Bring the soup to a boil, reduce to a simmer and cook for 60 minutes.

If you're using a slow cooker, set it on low and add all the ingredients before you go to work. Let it cook for about 9 hours. You'll have a delicious meal cooked to perfection when you get home.

Cut tortillas into strips and bake for 12 minutes at 350 degrees, until crisp. To serve the soup, ladle into bowls and garnish with tortilla strips, lime and avocado.

Enchilada Sauce

Makes 5 cups

This freezes well, so make a double batch and keep some on hand for future use!

1 tablespoon olive oil

1 small yellow onion, diced

3 cloves garlic, minced

1 teaspoon chopped fresh oregano

1/4 teaspoon ground cinnamon

1 teaspoon ground cumin

5 tablespoons chili powder

5 cups chicken stock (see page 10), divided

1 ounce semisweet chocolate

3 tablespoons cornstarch

In a medium-sized saucepot over medium heat, add the olive oil and sauté the onion until translucent. Add the garlic, oregano, cinnamon, and cumin and sauté for 2 minutes. Slowly stir in the chili powder. Add 4 $1/2$ cups chicken stock, saving the remainder to mix with the cornstarch. Add the chocolate and cook over medium heat for 20 minutes, then reduce heat to a simmer. Make a cornstarch slurry by combining the cornstarch with the remaining $1/2$ cup chicken stock. Blend the slurry until smooth and then whisk into the sauce. If needed, continue cooking until sauce has reduced a little. If desired, add more chocolate to taste.

Frogmore Stew

This is perfect for serving a crowd outside. Have crab crackers and plenty of cocktail sauce and napkins on hand, as well as lots of warm garlic butter for the corn and potatoes. Leftover shells and corncobs can go right on the table, and when everyone is done, just roll up the newspapers and toss them in the trash. Presto! Cleanup is a snap.

3 gallons water

1 Meyer lemon, quartered

1 cup Carolina Bay seasoning (recipe follows)

2 Vidalia onions, quartered

24 small new potatoes

4 ears Silver Queen corn or yellow corn, cut crosswise into 2-inch pieces

3/4 pounds kielbasa sausage, cut crosswise into 1/2 inch pieces

2 dozen clams, scrubbed

2 pounds large shrimp, unpeeled, heads and tails on

8 whole blue crabs, or 8 stone crab claws

In a large stock pot big enough to hold all the ingredients (a turkey cooker with a basket works great), bring the water to a boil. Add the lemon and Carolina Bay seasoning. Lower the heat to a high simmer. Begin adding ingredients at 7-minute intervals, starting with the onions and potatoes. Cook for 7 minutes, and then add the corn, sausage and clams. Cook for another 7 minutes, and then add the shrimp and the whole crab or claws. Let the pot go for 7 more minutes. Strain the liquid from the stew and transfer to separate serving pans. You can also just serve right in the pot; set it on a large table covered with newspaper and dig in.

Carolina Bay Seasoning

8 dried bay leaves

1/4 cup mustard seeds

3 tablespoons coriander seeds

2 tablespoons whole allspice

2 tablespoons dill seed

1 teaspoon whole cloves

1 dried jalapeño

1 teaspoon marjoram

1 teaspoon dried grated lemon zest

2 teaspoons black peppercorns

2 teaspoons paprika

2 teaspoons ground ginger

1 teaspoon granulated garlic

1 teaspoon crushed red pepper

In a spice grinder, grind all the ingredients above. Store in an airtight container.

Minorcan Clam Chowder

Serves 8 to 10

Growing up in St Augustine, Florida, we made a spicy tomato-based chowder called Minorcan Clam Chowder. Back in 1768, eight ships set sail from Spain's Minorca Isle with 1,500 people on board, heading to a plantation near New Smyrna Beach, Florida. But the trip took a turn for the worse when the voyagers discovered that their destination was a slave plantation owned by Dr. Andrew Turnbull. They were held there for 9 years. Some captives escaped and settled in St. Augustine, where they were protected under the administration of Governor Patrick Tonyn. St. Augustine was founded by Spaniards in 1565, so it was a natural haven for the Minorcan voyagers and their spicy Mediterranean style of cooking.

This chowder gets its kick from the datil pepper that is grown in the area. Two friends that I grew up with in St. Augustine, Chris Way and Beanie Masters, are lifelong residents and restaurateurs. Chris pickles the peppers and makes a great datil hot sauce. The hot sauce is sold as the Dat'l Do-It brand and is available in grocery stores and online. Beanie was the first person who taught me how to make chowder. For more heat, you can add additional datil peppers, and if you have trouble finding datils, substitute habanero peppers.

1 teaspoon olive oil

$^1/_2$ pound salt pork or bacon, finely diced

1 large yellow onion, diced

1 cup diced celery

1 cup diced red bell pepper

1 cup diced green bell pepper

2 datil peppers, chopped

$^1/_2$ cup diced carrots

1 clove garlic, crushed and minced

1 (28-ounce) can crushed tomatoes, or 4–5 vine-ripened tomatoes, peeled, seeded and chopped

1 (15-ounce) can tomato purée

2 teaspoons minced fresh thyme

1 teaspoon dried basil

$^1/_2$ teaspoon chopped fresh oregano

3 dried bay leaves, divided

1 teaspoon marjoram leaves

1 pound potatoes, cubed

3 cups water

1 lemon quarter

1 bag farm-raised cherrystone clams, scrubbed and washed, or 1 pound canned chopped clams

3 cups water or bottled clam juice

Coarse sea salt and freshly ground black pepper

Crackers

Hot sauce

In a large heavy-bottomed pot over medium heat, add the olive oil and sauté the salt pork or bacon until browned. Add the onion, celery, peppers, and carrots and sauté until tender. Add the garlic, tomatoes, tomato purée, thyme, basil, oregano, 2 bay leaves, and marjoram and cook over low heat.

In another pot, cover the potatoes with salted water and bring to a boil. Cook for 5 minutes, drain, and then add the potatoes to the tomato and vegetable mixture.

If using fresh clams, place a large pot on the stove filled with the water, the lemon quarter and the remaining 1 bay leaf. Use a steamer basket to add the clams to the pot, or just place them directly in the pot if you don't have a basket. Steam until the clams have all opened. Remove the clams and the lemon from the pot, saving the liquid for the chowder. Remove the clams from the shells, chop roughly and add to the tomato and potato mixture. Strain the clam juice through a fine strainer and add to the tomato and clam mixture. You should have about 3 to 4 cups of liquid. Add 3 cups to start and use the last cup if you prefer thinner soup. Cook for 5 minutes more.

If using chopped clams, add them to the chowder after the potatoes and substitute bottled clam juice.

Check for seasoning, adding salt and pepper as desired. Serve hot with crackers and hot sauce.

She Crab Soup

Serves 6 to 8

1/4 pound (1 stick) butter

1 cup all-purpose flour

1/2 cup peeled and finely diced carrots

1 1/2 cups finely diced yellow onions

1 cup finely diced celery

1 tablespoon Worcestershire sauce

1 tablespoon Texas Pete hot sauce

1 chicken bouillon cube

1/2 teaspoon ground mace

1/2 teaspoon coarse sea salt, plus more for seasoning

1/4 teaspoon freshly ground black pepper, plus more for seasoning

2 cups clam juice

4 cups milk

1 cup heavy cream

1 pound crabmeat, picked for shells

2 tablespoons crab roe, picked for shells

2 hard-boiled eggs, chopped

1/4 cup minced green onion

Paprika

Fino sherry

In medium-sized soup pot over medium heat, melt the butter. When the butter bubbles and begins to froth, whisk in the flour and cook for 5 minutes, stirring often with a wooden spoon. Continue stirring and browning the flour until the color changes from white to blond. You now have a blond roux. Stir in the carrots, onions, and celery and cook for 5 minutes. Add the Worcestershire sauce, hot sauce, bouillon cube, mace, salt and pepper. Cook for 5 minutes, then add the clam juice, milk and cream. Bring to a boil and reduce heat to a simmer. Cook for 15 minutes, add the crabmeat and roe, and cook for an additional 15 minutes. Check for seasoning and add salt and pepper as needed.

Pour the soup into bowls and garnish with the egg, green onion, and a pinch of paprika. Top the soup with a dash of sherry and serve.

Oyster Stew with Spinach and Wild Mushroom Cakes

Serves 4

Carolina Cups are locally harvested oysters in the Beaufort/May River area. If you can't find these, substitute your favorite local oyster.

1 1/2 tablespoons of unsalted butter, divided

1 tablespoon chopped garlic

1 medium shallot, diced

1 tablespoon finely chopped chives

3/4 cup licorice-flavored liqueur or Pernod

2/3 cups heavy cream

1/2 pint Carolina Cup oysters with juice

Sea salt and cracked black pepper

4 wild mushroom and spinach cakes (recipe follows)

Fried spinach (optional, recipe follows)

Place a medium-sized saucepan over medium-high heat until hot. Add 1 tablespoon of butter and melt. Add the garlic and shallot and cook for about 45 seconds, or until golden brown. Add the chives and cook for about 30 seconds. Carefully add the liqueur or Pernod. The pan will briefly flame. Continue cooking until the flame dies out. Add the heavy cream and reduce the mixture by half, cooking for about 2 minutes.

Add the oysters and cook just until the edges begin to curl. Remove the pan from heat and swirl in the remaining $^1/_2$ tablespoon butter. Set the pan off to the side and season with salt and pepper. Keep warm.

Place equal amounts of the oyster stew into 4 bowls, then place the wild mushroom and spinach cake in the middle of the bowl. Garnish with fried spinach if desired.

Wild Mushroom and Spinach Cakes

Serves 4

This flavorful recipe calls for wild mushrooms, but go ahead and substitute a mix of domestic mushrooms if you can't find wild ones. Be sure to wash and clean them thoroughly.

2 tablespoons unsalted butter

1 medium shallot, diced

2 tablespoons minced garlic

1 $^1/_2$ cups wild mushrooms (such as lobster, morels or chanterelles), cleaned and sliced

1 (10-ounce) package frozen spinach, thawed, drained and chopped

$^1/_2$ pint of Carolina Cup oysters with juice

$^1/_2$ cup fresh bread crumbs

1 large egg, beaten

$^1/_2$ cup White Lily Self-Rising flour

2 tablespoons canola oil

Place a medium skillet over medium-high heat until hot. Add the butter and sauté the shallot and garlic until golden brown. Add the mushrooms and sauté until cooked through. Add the chopped spinach and cook for about 1 minute, then add the oysters and cook until the edges start to curl. Transfer the mixture to a bowl and chill for about 45 minutes. After the mixture chills, stir in the bread crumbs and egg.

Place the flour in a shallow bowl. Form the chilled mushroom and oyster mixture into 4 separate balls and shape like you would a crab cake, about 1 inch thick. Dredge the cakes in the flour.

Place a large skillet over medium-high heat. Add the canola oil and heat until hot but not smoking. Sauté the cakes for about 2 minutes per side, or until cooked through and golden brown.

Fried Spinach

Makes 4 portions

4 ounces spinach

Vegetable or canola oil for frying

Salt and freshly ground black pepper

Heat oil in a fryer to 325 degrees. Fry the spinach until crispy. Remove the spinach from the fryer and place on paper towels to absorb any excess oil. Season with salt and pepper.

Summer Minestrone

Serves 6 to 8

$^1/_2$ cup olive oil

1 carrot, medium diced

$^3/_4$ cup yellow onion, chopped

2 cloves garlic, crushed and chopped

1 zucchini, medium diced

1 yellow squash, medium diced

1 fennel bulb, medium diced

$^1/_4$ cup chopped fresh basil

$^1/_8$ cup chopped fresh oregano

3 cups peeled, seeded and diced tomatoes

2 cups tomato juice

6 cups chicken stock (see page 10)

1 chicken bouillon cube

1 tablespoon sugar

$^1/_2$ cup fresh or frozen spinach, chopped

$^1/_2$ cup fresh or frozen green peas

3 cups cooked garbanzo beans

1 cup grated Parmesan cheese, plus more for garnish

Coarse sea salt and cracked black pepper

1 cup orzo pasta

$^1/_4$ cup chopped fresh parsley

In a large, heavy-bottomed pot over medium heat, heat the olive oil. Sauté the carrot, onion, garlic, zucchini and squash until the onion is translucent. Stir in the basil and oregano. Add the tomatoes, tomato juice, chicken stock, bouillon cube and sugar. Continue to cook over medium-high heat for 20 minutes. Add the spinach, green peas, and garbanzo beans and bring to a boil. Skim any froth, add the Parmesan and check the seasoning, adding salt and pepper as needed. Remove the pot from heat and allow to cool.

Cook the orzo pasta according to package directions. Divide the orzo among the bowls and ladle the soup on top. Garnish with Parmesan and chopped parsley.

SANDWICHES
& SOUTHWEST

Fried Green Tomato BLT

Makes 4 sandwiches

This one is on the menu, and now it's made with pimiento cheese and toasted jalapeño cornbread. We used to make the bread here at the restaurant, but now I have an artisan bread company that provides it fresh from the oven. It's a combination of wheat, malted barley flour and corn flour, with dried ground jalapeños. Corn flour has no gluten, so it has to be mixed with flour or used strictly to make unleavened bread such as Pan Meino.

2 tablespoons butter, melted

8 slices toasted jalapeño cornbread (recipe below, or store-bought)

2 cups pimiento cheese (pages 54–57)

16 slices Nueske's applewood-smoked bacon, cooked

12 slices fried green tomatoes (see page 46)

1 head red leaf lettuce, chilled

Butter and griddle both sides of the bread. Spread a thin layer of pimiento cheese on one side of each piece of bread. Lay the pimiento cheese sides up and top half of the slices with 3 slices fried green tomatoes, 4 slices bacon and 3 red leaf lettuce leaves. Place the remaining slices of bread on top, pimiento cheese side down. Carefully cut the sandwich in half using a serrated knife. Place a toothpick in each half to hold it together. Enjoy.

Jalapeño Yeast Cornbread

Makes 2 loaves

If you want to make your own jalapeño cornbread use the standard bread-making method for this one.

4 teaspoons yeast

$1/4$ cup lukewarm water

$1/3$ teaspoon salt

1 tablespoon sugar

$1/4$ cup lard

1 tablespoon malt extract

$1/8$ cup dried ground jalapeños

4 $1/2$ cups unbleached enriched flour

1 cup degerminated yellow corn meal

Dissolve yeast in water. Mix all ingredients together, knead, and cover dough to let rise until double in size. Punch down and shape in loaf pans. Let it rise again until double in size. Bake at 400 degrees F for 25 minutes. Score the top and bake 10 more minutes.

Oyster Sliders on King's Hawaiian Rolls with Brussels Sprouts Slaw

Serves 6 to 8

24 small King's Hawaiian rolls

$1/2$ cup butter, melted

2 cups Brussels sprouts slaw (recipe follows)

24 fried oysters (recipe follows)

$3/4$ cup South Carolina mustard sauce (see page 24) or store-bought barbecue sauce

24 sweet grass toothpicks

Slice the rolls in half and brush both sides with butter. Toast in a medium-hot pan or on a griddle. Keep warm. Place a large spoonful of slaw on the bottom of each roll, top with a fried oyster, and then finish with barbecue sauce. Put the tops of the buns on the oysters and decorate with a sweetgrass toothpick. Put 3 sliders onto each plate.

Fried Oysters

Makes 4 dozen

2 cups buttermilk

2 $^1/_3$ cups cornmeal

2 $^1/_3$ cups all-purpose flour

1 tablespoon Creole seasoning (see page 23)

1 tablespoon coarse sea salt

1 pint Carolina Cups or your favorite local oysters

Vegetable or canola oil for frying

Line a sheet tray with wax paper and set aside. Pour the buttermilk into a medium-sized bowl. In another bowl, combine the cornmeal, flour, Creole seasoning and salt, mixing well. Drain the oysters and place them in the buttermilk. Remove the oysters one at a time, allowing the excess buttermilk to run back into the bowl. Dredge the oysters in the cornmeal mixture, making sure they are well covered. Transfer to wax paper–lined sheet tray until all the oysters are breaded and ready to fry.

Line a plate with paper towels and set aside. In a heavy-bottomed skillet with high sides and fitted with a thermometer, bring at least 2 inches of oil to 375 degrees F. Working in batches of 6, fry the oysters until golden brown, about 1 $^1/_2$ minutes. Using a slotted spoon, remove the oysters and drain on the paper towel–lined plate. Serve right away.

Brussels Sprouts Slaw

Serves 8

1 $^1/_2$ pounds Brussels sprouts

2 tablespoons white vinegar

$^3/_4$ cup Duke's mayonnaise

2 tablespoons sour cream

2 tablespoons grated red onion

2 tablespoons sugar, plus more as needed

1 tablespoon dry mustard

2 teaspoons celery salt

Coarse sea salt and freshly ground black pepper

Using a mandolin or a food processor fitted with a grater attachment, shred the Brussels sprouts and place them in a large bowl. In a medium-sized bowl, whisk together the vinegar, mayonnaise, sour cream, onion, sugar, mustard, and celery salt; season with salt and pepper. Add three-fourths of the dressing to the Brussels sprouts. Mix well to combine and taste for seasoning; add more dressing if needed, along with additional salt, pepper or sugar if desired.

The Steak Sandwich

Serves 4

This is the king of steak sandwiches. From time to time, I've been known to top it with foie gras and black truffles, but that's getting a little too fancy.

2 tablespoons olive oil, divided

1 1/2 pounds beef tenderloin, cut into 4 medallions pounded lightly to 1/2 inch thickness

Salt and freshly ground black pepper

4 (2-ounce) slices cheese of choice

4 bread rolls, cut open lengthwise

1 large Vidalia onion, sliced and caramelized

8 thick slices good-quality bacon, cooked

Mustard-Mayo (recipe follows)

Sliced tomato (optional)

Lettuce leaves (optional)

Start the grill or place a skillet over high heat until piping hot. Drizzle 1 tablespoon olive oil over the meat, season with salt and pepper, and rub in. Place the meat into the hot pan. Cook for about 3 minutes on each side, or longer for well done. Remove the steaks from the pan, top with cheese and let rest. Place the rolls in the skillet and toast lightly for a few seconds.

Spread the mustard-mayo on both halves of the rolls and place a steak on each bottom bun. Top with 2 slices bacon and one-fourth of the caramelized onion. If you need some vegetables to feel better about all of this deliciousness, add an obligatory slice of tomato and a little lettuce. Now you can enjoy the sandwich guilt free.

Mustard-Mayo

Makes 1 1/2 cups

1 raw egg

2 tablespoons Dijon mustard

2 tablespoons whole grain mustard

2 tablespoons apple cider vinegar

1 clove garlic, crushed

1/2 teaspoon sugar

1/2 teaspoon sea salt

1 1/2 cups (12 ounces) canola oil

In the bowl of a food processor, add the egg, Dijon and whole grain mustards, vinegar, garlic, sugar and salt. Start the processor and slowly add the oil in a small stream. Once the

mayonnaise is thick, transfer to an airtight container or use right away. Keeps up to 1 week in the refrigerator.

Lump Crab BLT

We serve two delicious versions of southern BLTs. This one earned an honorable mention for the best sandwich in America by Restaurant Hospitality *magazine in 2014. The simple trick to the lump crab BLT is the crab. Use only fresh lump crabmeat. Canned crab is strictly forbidden!*

1 pound jumbo lump crabmeat

$^1/_2$ cup Duke's mayonnaise, plus more as needed

Juice of 1 lemon

Salt and freshly ground black pepper

16 slices Nueske's applewood-smoked bacon

8 slices thick-cut whole wheat bread

12 slices fried green tomatoes (see page 46), warm

1 head red leaf lettuce, chilled

Place the crabmeat in a bowl and pick through for shells. Check one more time just to be sure you've got them all.

Transfer the well-picked crabmeat to a small bowl. Add the mayonnaise and lemon juice. If you like the mixture a little wetter, add a bit more mayonnaise. Mix gently and try not to break up the lumps of crabmeat. Season with a little salt and pepper; set aside.

Cook the bacon, remove from pan and keep warm.

Toast the bread and spread a layer of the crab mixture on each piece of toast. Top 4 slices of toast with 3 fried green tomatoes, 4 slices cooked bacon, and 3 red leaf lettuce leaves. Put the tops on and cut in half using a serrated knife. Try not to smash the sandwich—let the knife do the work. Place a toothpick in each half. Enjoy.

Grilled Flank Steak Tacos with Cherry Tomato and Mozzarella Salsa

Serves 6

1 1/2 cups red wine

1/2 cup olive oil

3 cloves garlic, minced

2 pounds flank steak

Salt and freshly ground black pepper

6 flour tortillas

6 corn tortillas

In a medium-sized bowl, combine the wine, olive oil and garlic to make the marinade. Season the flank steak with salt and pepper. Add the seasoned flank steak to a ziplock bag or baking dish. Pour the marinade over the steak and chill for at least 2 hours or overnight.

When ready to cook, get the grill hot and cook the steak for 4 minutes on one side and 2 minutes on the other. The flank steak should be rare to medium-rare. Remove from heat and allow to rest. Slice diagonally into very thin slices.

Warm the tortillas and top with 2 or 3 slices of the grilled steak and the salsa. Serve right away.

Cherry Tomato and Mozzarella Salsa

Makes 2 cups

1 pint cherry tomatoes, quartered

1 shallot, diced

2 fresh mozzarella balls, diced

1 tablespoon chopped fresh basil

2 teaspoons chopped fresh cilantro

2 teaspoons balsamic vinegar

1 tablespoon extra virgin olive oil

1 teaspoon minced garlic

Coarse sea salt and freshly ground black pepper

Mix all the ingredients together, check for seasoning and add salt and pepper to taste. Refrigerate in an airtight container.

Tom and Suzi Parsell having spent a lot of time in Taos, New Mexico, that, and with Suzi being from Dallas, we've added a lot of southwestern food items to the menu over the years. Going through the menus from the early years, I picked out a couple of my favorite recipes.

TACO SHELLS

I like to use a combination of soft, white and yellow corn flour tortillas. Just heat them quickly on the grill and place alternately in a cloth-lined basket to keep them warm. They're great for outdoor entertaining, quick and easy.

Grilled Vegetable Taco

Serves 6 to 8

1 red bell pepper, peeled and seeded, julienned

1 yellow pepper, peeled and seeded, julienned

1 red onion, sliced

4 portobello mushrooms, julienned

1 zucchini, sliced

1 clove garlic, crushed and minced

1/4 cup (2 ounces) balsamic vinegar

1/4 cup (2 ounces) extra virgin olive

6 flour tortillas

6 corn tortillas

Coarse sea salt and ground black pepper

Chipotle paste (see page 99)

4 ounces crumbled goat cheese

6 ounces arugula

Turn on the grill. Cook the peppers on the heated grill. When charred, place in a small bowl and cover with plastic wrap.

Grill the onion and the portobello mushrooms for about 7 minutes; remove from heat and keep warm. Grill the zucchini—it will be quick—about 1 minute per side. Remove the roasted peppers from the bowl; peel and seed.

Julienne all the vegetables, put into a medium-sized bowl and add the garlic, balsamic vinegar, and olive oil; season with salt and pepper to taste.

Warm the tortillas on the grill. Lay them on the counter and lightly paint with chipotle paste. Stuff the tortillas with grilled vegetables, goat cheese and arugula. Serve right away.

Grilled-Lamb Tacos with Apricots, Chipotle and Cucumber Salsa

Serves 6

2 lamb loins, silverskin removed

Salt and freshly ground black pepper

Chipotle paste (recipe follows), or store-bought

Apricot glaze (recipe follows) or store-bought preserves

6 flour tortillas

6 corn tortillas

Cucumber salsa (recipe follows)

Get the grill nice and hot and place the lamb loins on a sheet tray. Season the lamb with salt and pepper and brush each side with both the chipotle paste (lightly) and Apricot glaze. Grill the lamb loin over medium-high heat for about 4 minutes on one side and 2 minutes on the other, until medium-rare. Remove to a cutting board and let rest. Warm the tortillas on the grill and place in a cloth-lined basket to keep warm.

When ready to serve, brush the lamb loin one more time with the paste and glaze, and slice the meat about $1/4$ inch thick. Place meat in a tortilla and top with the cucumber salsa.

Apricot Glaze

Makes 1 1/2 cups

1 1/2 cups water

1 cup dried apricots

1/2 cup firmly packed brown sugar

2 tablespoons apple cider vinegar

2 teaspoons freshly squeezed lemon juice

1 teaspoon minced ginger

In a medium-sized saucepot, combine all the ingredients and bring to a boil. Reduce the heat and simmer for 15 minutes. Remove from heat and pulse in a food processor fitted with a metal blade until smooth. Allow to cool. Place in an airtight container and refrigerate.

Cucumber Salsa

Makes 3 cups

1 English (hothouse) cucumber, diced

3 Roma tomatoes, diced

1 red bell pepper, diced

2 serrano chile peppers, minced

1 small red onion, diced

1 clove garlic, crushed and minced

Juice of 2 limes

2 teaspoons chopped fresh mint

2 teaspoons chopped fresh basil

2 teaspoons chopped fresh dill

2 tablespoons red wine vinegar

2 tablespoons extra virgin olive oil

Coarse sea salt and freshly ground black pepper to taste

In a medium-sized bowl, combine all the ingredients and let sit for 30 minutes. Store in an airtight container and chill.

Chipotle Paste

Makes about 3/4 cup

1 1/2 cups water

1/3 cup loosely packed brown sugar, plus 1/8 cup molasses, combined

4 ounces dried chipotle chiles, 5-6 chiles

3 cloves garlic, or 1 tablespoon roasted garlic purée (see page 18)

Preheat the oven to 350 degrees F.

In a medium-sized saucepot over medium-high heat, bring the water to a boil; add the sugar and let it dissolve. Turn the heat down to a simmer.

Place the dried peppers on a sheet tray and bake until the peppers expand and puff up, about 15 minutes. Remove from the oven; they will be crispy. Remove the stems and seeds. In a food processor fitted with a metal blade, process the chiles until they turn to powder. Add the chiles and roasted garlic to the sugar and water mixture; let it reduce to a thick paste. Remove from heat and store in an airtight container. Freezes well.

Spicy Chicken Enchiladas with Green Chiles, Havarti Cheese and Tomato-Tomatillo Salsa

Serves 6

This is a tried-and-true version that has made its appearance on and off the menu for years. When the wait staff keeps pestering you to make them, it's got to be a good south-of-the-border truck stop special.

There are two ways to cook the chicken for these enchiladas, but the more correct way is to poach whole chickens in a court-bouillon of diced carrot, celery and onion with peppercorns and a bay leaf. The alternate and faster method is to coat the chicken breasts in olive oil and grill them, then cool and julienne. If you decide to use this method, you'll need to buy enough chicken broth for four cups, a couple of cans of tomato purée and two small cans of green chiles, skipping the preparation of the tomatoes and poblano chiles.

2 whole chickens, or 7 (8-ounce) chicken breasts

$^1/_2$ cup chopped carrot

$^1/_2$ cup chopped celery

1 cup chopped onion

2 dried bay leaves

1 tablespoon black peppercorns

$^1/_4$ cup olive oil

12 scallions, sliced

6 cloves garlic, crushed and minced

4 large ripe tomatoes, blanched, peeled, seeded and puréed, or 2 (6-ounce) cans tomato purée

4 cups reserved chicken stock or store-bought

4 poblano chiles, roasted, peeled, seeded and chopped, or 2 (4-ounce) cans diced green chiles

2 teaspoons chopped fresh basil

2 teaspoons chopped fresh oregano

2 teaspoons ground cumin

2 teaspoons coarse sea salt

4 cups grated Havarti cheese

4 cups grated cheddar cheese

24 corn tortillas

2 cups sour cream, plus more for garnish

2 cups tomato-tomatillo salsa (recipe follows)

IF USING WHOLE CHICKENS: Place the chicken in a large pot, and add the carrots, celery, onion, spices and water to cover. Bring the pot to a boil, then lower the heat to simmer. Cook for 30 minutes and remove the cooked chicken. Pick all the meat from the bones and dice. Reduce the liquid to about 4 cups.

IF USING CHICKEN BREASTS: Preheat the grill. Coat the chicken in $1/8$ cup olive oil and grill over medium-high heat until cooked through. Remove from the grill, let cool and julienne.

Preheat the oven to 350 degrees F. In a large skillet over medium-high heat, add the $1/4$ cup olive oil and sauté the scallions and garlic for 2 minutes. Add the homemade or canned tomato purée, the reserved or store-bought chicken stock, the poblano or green chiles, basil, oregano, cumin and salt. Reduce the heat to a simmer and cook for 10 minutes.

In a medium-sized bowl, mix the Havarti and cheddar cheese together; set aside. Dip the tortillas one by one into the tomato mixture to soften them and place on a baking pan or in an ovenproof dish. Equally divide the chicken among the tortillas and top with a good pinch of cheese, about 2 ounces. Roll up the tortillas and place seam side down on the baking pan or ovenproof dish, lining up the tortillas side by side. Pour one-third of the tomato sauce on top of the tortillas. Combine the sour cream with the remaining tomato sauce, pour over tortillas and top with the remaining cheese. Wrap with foil and bake for 30 minutes. Garnish with the salsa and a dollop of sour cream.

Tomato-Tomatillo Salsa

Makes 2 cups

5–6 tomatillos, husked and rinsed

2 tablespoons olive oil, divided

1 small yellow onion, chopped

1 clove garlic, chopped

1 cup chicken stock (see page 10)

3 tablespoons fresh chopped cilantro (about 12 stems)

2 plum tomatoes, chopped

2 serrano chiles, stemmed

Coarse sea salt and pepper

1 lime

In a large skillet over medium-high heat, pan roast the tomatillos until blistered and charred. Remove from pan, allow to cool and peel. Return the pan to the heat, add 1 tablespoon olive oil and sauté the onion until caramelized. Add the garlic and cook for 1 minute. Remove the skillet from heat. In a food processor fitted with a metal blade, pulse the onions, garlic, and charred tomatillos for just a few seconds—the mixture should be coarse. Pour the mixture back into the pan and add the remaining 1 tablespoon olive oil. Cook over medium heat for 7 minutes, add the chicken stock and reduce the heat to a low simmer for 10 minutes. Add the cilantro, tomatoes and serrano chiles. Check for seasoning and add salt and pepper to taste. Add a squeeze of lime juice, remove from heat and chill until ready to use.

PASTA, EGGS & GRITS

Stone-Ground White Grits

Yields 4 to 6 servings

White grits come to us from a lush green cove in the farmlands of scenic Belvidere, Tennessee. Falls Mill, operated by John and Jane Lovett, has been supplying white grits to Magnolias for 25 years. The mill began as a cotton and wool factory in 1873 and was converted to a cotton gin and then a woodworking shop before being restored to a grain mill. The three-story brick structure and mill is water powered by Factory Creek. Today's water wheel is 108 years old, 32 feet tall and 4 feet wide. These good old-fashioned grits are ground at Falls Mill using a process that dates back to the nineteenth century.

3 cups water

1 teaspoon kosher salt, plus more

1 cup grits

2 tablespoons butter

1 cup heavy cream or milk

Freshly ground pepper

Place the water and 1 teaspoon salt in a medium-sized saucepan over medium-high heat; bring to a boil. Add the grits and stir frequently. Let the grits come back to a boil, reduce the heat to low and cook for 45 minutes. Add butter and cream, add salt and pepper to taste and serve warm.

"It's the texture of these grits that sets them apart. We mill corn fresh each week to produce superior grits that are shipped on the same day they're milled. We supply several hundred pounds of grits to Magnolias each month and count them as our oldest and best customer. Here's to 25 more years of exceptional southern cuisine."

—John and Jane Lovett

Tagliatelle with Broccoli Rabe, Chickpeas and Pecorino

Serves 4 to 6

The good thing about most pasta dishes is that they are quick to prepare. This recipe makes an easy lunch or dinner.

1–1 1/2 pounds fresh tagliatelle pasta

1/2 cup extra virgin olive oil

12 ounces broccoli rabe, blanched and chopped

1/2 pound cooked chickpeas

1 tablespoon freshly squeezed lemon juice

Zest of 2 lemons

1/2 cup grated pecorino cheese, plus more for garnish

Coarse sea salt and ground black pepper

Pinch of red pepper flakes

Cook pasta in boiling water, drain and keep warm. In a sauté pan heat half of the olive oil, then quickly add the broccoli rabe and sauté for 3 minutes. Add the chickpeas, lemon juice and zest and warm thoroughly. Add the cooked pasta, cheese, and salt and pepper to taste. Drizzle a little olive oil on top. Serve with additional grated cheese and red pepper flakes.

Bow Tie Pasta with Chicken, Broccolini and Bacon

Serves 4 to 6

1 pound bow tie pasta

3 tablespoons olive oil

4 large boneless chicken thighs, cut into strips

5 slices applewood-smoked bacon, chopped

2 cloves garlic, crushed and minced

2 cups Broccolini, blanched

1 1/2 cups heavy cream

Sea salt and ground black pepper

1 cup shredded Parmesan cheese

1/4 cup chopped fresh basil

Cook pasta according to package directions in boiling salted water, then drain.

Heat the olive oil in a medium-sized sauté pan over medium heat and cook the chicken thighs and bacon about 5 to 6 minutes, or until the chicken is golden brown and cooked through. Add the garlic to the pan and cook for 1 minute. Add the blanched Broccolini and cream and warm thoroughly. Pour the sauce over the pasta and season to taste with salt and pepper. Top with cheese and chopped basil.

Eggs Benedict, Country Fried Steak, Poached Eggs, Green Chile and Cheddar Southern Waffles and Sausage Gravy *Serves 6*

This combination is one of my absolute favorite breakfasts. It's perfect on a weekend when you have time to linger over coffee and savor every single bite. But be forewarned, this may put you down for a nap with a full belly and a smile on your face. The yard work will have to wait. The waffle batter works best made a day ahead and allowed to stand in the refrigerator overnight.

SAUSAGE GRAVY

$1/2$ pound breakfast sausage

3 tablespoons unsalted butter

2 tablespoons all-purpose flour

2 cups milk

1 teaspoon coarse sea salt

$3/4$ teaspoon ground black pepper

GREEN CHILE AND CHEDDAR WAFFLES

2 cups White Lily Self-Rising flour

2 teaspoons baking powder

$1/4$ cup yellow cornmeal

$3/4$ teaspoon baking soda

1 teaspoon sugar

1 teaspoon fine sea salt

1 egg, beaten

2 cups buttermilk

1 (7-ounce) can green chiles, drained

1 cup grated cheddar cheese

$1/2$ cup (1 stick) butter, melted

COUNTRY FRIED STEAK

3 cups all-purpose flour

1 teaspoon smoked paprika

1 teaspoon baking soda

2 teaspoons baking powder

$1 1/2$ teaspoons ground black pepper

1 tablespoon coarse sea salt

1 teaspoons granulated garlic

3 cups buttermilk

2 tablespoons Texas Pete hot sauce

1 egg

6 slices cube steak

Oil for frying

POACHED EGGS

12 large eggs

1 teaspoon white vinegar (optional)

SAUSAGE GRAVY: In a heavy-bottomed skillet over medium heat, brown the sausage in the butter for about 5 minutes. Remove sausage and drain the oil from the pan, reserving 2 tablespoons in the pan. Add the flour to the pan, whisking until it is well incorporated, about 2 minutes. Add the milk to the pan and keep whisking until you have a smooth, creamy gravy. Stir in the salt and pepper and add the sausage back to the gravy. Remove from heat and keep warm.

GREEN CHILE AND CHEDDAR WAFFLES: Mix and sift all dry ingredients together in a large bowl. Add beaten egg, buttermilk, chiles, cheese and melted butter. Combine carefully, folding in rather than beating. If you refrigerated the batter overnight, warm up a bit before heating up the waffle iron.

COUNTRY FRIED STEAK: In a shallow pan or bowl place the all-purpose flour, paprika, baking soda, baking powder, pepper, salt and garlic and mix well.

In another bowl combine the buttermilk, hot sauce and egg; mix well.

Place the cube steaks in the flour mixture and coat well, shaking off any excess flour. Next dip the steaks into the egg-and-buttermilk mixture, then dredge in the flour a second time to coat the steaks thoroughly.

Heat the oil in a large, deep skillet over medium-high heat and carefully fry 2 to 3 steaks at a time, depending on the size of the skillet. Cook until golden brown, about 3 minutes per side. Remove from pan and keep warm.

POACHED EGGS: In a large saucepan add $1 \frac{1}{2}$ inches of water and bring to a high simmer. If your eggs are very fresh, you can skip the vinegar, but if the eggs are a few days old or more, add a teaspoon of white vinegar to the poaching water. Turn the heat to low. Cook eggs 4 at a time. Crack each egg into an individual cup, then carefully pour the eggs from the cups into the simmering water. Poach to desired doneness, leaving the eggs soft. Remove eggs with a slotted spoon and keep warm.

TO SERVE: Place a waffle on each plate. Top with country fried steak and ladle a generous amount of sausage gravy over the steak. Top with 2 poached eggs and serve piping hot.

Fried Egg and Country Ham on Sourdough Toast

Serves 4

After a busy day in the kitchen, this is one of my favorite late-night sandwiches. I can't say that it's healthy, but it sure hits the spot when you're hungry.

8 slices country ham, thinly sliced

8 slices sourdough bread, toasted

2 tablespoons melted butter

8 eggs

$\frac{1}{2}$ cup Duke's mayonnaise

16 slices heirloom tomatoes

8 slices white cheddar cheese

In a nonstick skillet over medium-high heat, sear the country ham and keep warm. Toast the bread. Cook the eggs to the temperature of your liking. Spread some mayonnaise on each slice of toast, topping with tomato, cheese, fried egg and ham. Use a sharp serrated knife to cut sandwich from corner to corner.

Dutch Oven French Toast with Apples, Country Sausage and Mascarpone Cheese

Serves 4 to 6

8 eggs

1 quart heavy cream

1 teaspoon ground cinnamon

2 tablespoons vanilla extract

1 dozen croissants

10 tablespoons butter, divided

2 cans apple pie filling

1 cup packed brown sugar, divided

1 pound breakfast sausage, cooked and crumbled

8 ounces mascarpone cheese

3 green apples, diced

The night before, whisk together the eggs, cream, cinnamon and vanilla in a large bowl. Set aside and refrigerate. Cut croissants into cubes and allow to dry overnight.

Lay croissants in a large baking dish, pour the egg mixture over and allow the bread to absorb the liquid. Using a slotted spoon, remove soaked croissants and reserve remaining custard in the same dish.

Preheat the oven to 350 degrees F. Butter the bottom of a Dutch oven with 4 tablespoons of butter. Add the pie filling and spread $1/2$ cup of brown sugar on top. Start layering the pan with $1/3$ of the croissant cubes, $1/2$ of the sausage and dot with $1/2$ of the cheese. Sprinkle with brown sugar and add $1/3$ of the apples. Start another layer of $1/3$ of the croissants cubes and 4 tablespoons butter, cubed. Sprinkle with remaining $1/2$ of sausage, $1/4$ cup of brown sugar, $1/3$ of the diced apples and remaining $1/2$ of the cheese. Finish the top layer with the remaining croissants, apples, 2 tablespoons butter and $1/4$ cup brown sugar. Pour any leftover custard over the top. Place in the oven covered with the lid and bake for 30 to 40 minutes, or until set. Wait about 10 minutes before cutting. Serve with your favorite maple syrup.

Lobster Corn Cakes with Steamed Asparagus, Crispy Bacon, Poached Eggs and Lobster Hollandaise Sauce

Serves 6

3 whole lobsters (approximately 1 1/4 pounds each), cooked and meat removed from shell

6 corn and lobster cakes (meat from above lobsters, recipe follows)

12 slices applewood-smoked bacon, cooked

1 pound asparagus (24 spears), blanched

6 eggs, poached (see page 107)

2 cups lobster hollandaise (recipe follows)

ORDER OF PREPARATION: Cook the lobsters and extract the meat (see How to Steam a Lobster, facing). Make the lobster corn cakes and reserve warm. Cook the bacon and reserve warm. Blanch the asparagus spears and reserve warm. Make the hollandaise and reserve warm. Poach the eggs.

TO ASSEMBLE: Place 1 corn and lobster cake on each plate and top with 2 thick slices of bacon, 4 spears of asparagus, and a poached egg. Finish with a generous ladle of lobster hollandaise. Serve hot.

Lobster Corn Cakes

Makes 6 cakes

3/4 cup white cornmeal

2/3 cup White Lily Self-Rising flour

1/2 tablespoon Rumford baking powder

1/4 cup diced red bell pepper

2 1/2 cups sweet corn

1/2 cup chopped green onions

1/2 cup milk

3 large eggs, beaten

2 cups lobster meat

Coarse sea salt and ground black pepper

3 eggs whites (1/4 cup), whipped to soft peaks

1 tablespoon olive oil

In a large bowl add the cornmeal, flour, baking powder, bell pepper, corn and onions and mix well. Add milk, eggs, lobster meat, and salt and pepper to taste; mix well. Fold in the whipped egg whites and set aside.

Lightly oil and heat a griddle until medium hot. Use a large kitchen spoon or scoop to form cakes and place them on the hot griddle. Cook for 3 minutes on each side, or until done. Remove from heat and place on a sheet tray or platter and keep warm.

Lobster Hollandaise

Serves 6

4 egg yolks

1 tablespoon lemon juice

1/4 teaspoon fine sea salt

3 dashes Tabasco sauce

2 1/2 tablespoons water

1 pound unsalted butter, melted

1 cup chopped cooked lobster meat

2 tablespoons chopped chives

Place the egg yolks, lemon juice, salt, Tabasco sauce and water in a glass or stainless steel mixing bowl. Place it over a pot of hot water, double-boiler style. The water should not touch the bottom of the bowl. Whisk the mixture vigorously until it doubles in volume. Be careful not to let the eggs get too hot or they will scramble. Slowly drizzle in the melted butter and continue whisking until the mixture doubles in volume again and is thick and creamy. Remove from heat and add the lobster and chives. Check for seasoning and add more lemon juice, Tabasco sauce, and salt if needed. Cover and keep warm until ready to use. If the sauce gets too thick, whisk in a few drops of warm water before serving.

{ HOW TO STEAM A LOBSTER }

Lobsters will yield approximately 27 percent of their overall weight when cooked and the meat is removed. These three lobsters will yield close to a pound of delicious meat. Place a large 4-to-5- gallon pot on the stove and fill about 2 inches deep with water. Add 2 teaspoons of coarse sea salt. Set a steaming rack inside if you have one. If not, just put the lobsters right in the pot. Bring the water to a rapid boil over high heat and add the lobsters. Put a lid on top and steam for 8 minutes. Carefully remove the lid and remove the lobsters, and quickly submerge them in cold water.

When the lobsters are cool enough to handle, remove the claws and tails. Lightly tap the claws on their sides with a mallet to barely crack the shells. Remove the claw meat, trying to keep it intact as much as possible. Place each lobster on its stomach, give the tail a quick twist and tug to remove the tail. Use kitchen shears to cut and split the length of the tail, remove the meat, place in bowl and refrigerate. Freeze the shells for later use.

Shellfish over Grits with Lobster Sauce, Tomato Concassé, Creamy White Grits *Serves 6*

3 whole lobsters, 1 1/4 pounds each

3 tablespoons butter

3 tablespoons shallots, minced

1 pound large sea scallops

1 pound large shrimp, peeled and deveined

1 pound reserved lobster meat, tail and claws cut into bite-size pieces

2 1/2 cups Lobster Sauce (recipe follows)

1/2 pound jumbo lump crabmeat

Salt and ground black pepper

8 cups creamy white grits (see page 115)

3 ounces fried spinach (see page 85)

3 tablespoons brunoise tomatoes (or diced)

LOBSTERS: See page 111 on how to steam a lobster. Reserve meat and refrigerate until ready to use. Reserve shells separately and cooking liquid separately.

TO FINISH: Melt butter in a large pot, making sure not to brown. Add the shallots and cook until translucent. Add the scallops and shrimp and cook over low heat for 2 to 3 minutes, until the scallops are firm but still a little translucent in the center. The shrimp should be pink. Be careful not to overcook. Add the lobster meat and sauté until warm. Add the Lobster Sauce and lump crabmeat and heat throughout. Check

salt and pepper and remove from heat. Divide the grits among 6 bowls and equally divide the shellfish on top. Top with remaining lobster sauce and garnish with the fried spinach and tomatoes. Serve immediately.

Lobster Sauce

Makes 2 1/2 cups

3 tablespoons unsalted butter, divided

1/4 cup all-purpose flour

2 cups lobster stock (recipe follows)

1/2 cup heavy cream

1/2 teaspoon paprika

1 tablespoon brandy

Fine sea salt

White pepper

Pinch of cayenne pepper

Heat 2 tablespoons of butter in a saucepan. Be sure not to brown it. Stir in the flour and cook over low heat for 2 minutes, stirring. Add half of the Lobster Stock and whisk continuously to make a smooth paste. Add the remaining stock and whisk until smooth. Add the cream, paprika, and brandy and simmer over low heat for 10 to 15 minutes, whisking occasionally. Stir in the remaining butter and season to taste with salt, white pepper and cayenne pepper. Remove from heat and allow to cool slightly. Cover with plastic wrap; this will prevent a film from forming over the sauce. Reserve until ready to use.

Lobster Stock

Makes 2 cups

4 tablespoons light olive oil

3/4 cup chopped onion

3/4 cup chopped celery

1/2 cup chopped carrot

2 cloves garlic, smashed

3 sprigs fresh tarragon

6 leaves fresh basil

2 dried bay leaves

4 black peppercorns, crushed

1 teaspoon fine sea salt

Reserved lobster shells

1 (6-ounce) can tomato paste

Reserved liquid from cooking lobsters, plus enough water to make 8 cups

In a heavy-bottomed pot, heat the oil and add the onion, celery, and carrot. Cook over low heat until the vegetables are soft but not caramelized. Add the garlic, tarragon, basil, bay leaves, peppercorns, and salt and cook for a minute. Add the lobster shells and crush the bodies by using a spoon or the end of a mallet. This releases the juices from the body cavity. Add the tomato paste and coat the shells. Continue to cook until the liquid has been reduced by half. The mixture should be pasty.

Add the lobster cooking liquid and water and bring slowly to a simmer. Discard any foam that rises to the top, and simmer for 35 minutes. When cool enough to handle, strain the stock through a fine sieve, pressing the solids to extract the maximum amount of stock.

Place the stock in a saucepan, bring to a boil, and reduce it to 2 cups to concentrate the flavor. Allow to cool to room temperature.

Spicy Shrimp and Sausage, Chicken Gravy, Creamy White Grits

Serves 6

1/2 pound spicy Italian sausage

1 tablespoon light olive oil

2 pounds medium or large shrimp, peeled and deveined

1 cup chicken stock, plus 1/2 cup if needed (see page 10)

Chicken gravy (recipe follows)

1/2 cup tasso ham, thinly sliced into 1-inch strips

2 tablespoons finely chopped parsley, divided

Creamy white grits (recipe follows)

Preheat the oven to 375 degrees F. Place the sausage on a baking sheet with raised sides and bake on the top oven rack for 10 to 15 minutes, or until it is firm and juices run clear. Allow to cool then cut into small bite-sized pieces. Set aside.

Over medium heat in a heavy-bottomed frying pan, heat the olive oil. Add the sausage and sauté for 2 minutes to brown slightly. Add the shrimp and sauté until they just begin to turn pink, not longer than 1 minute. Add 1 cup of the chicken stock to deglaze the pan. Add the chicken gravy, tasso and a tablespoon of parsley. Bring to a gentle boil and simmer for a minute while stirring. If needed, you can add the remaining chicken stock to thin the gravy.

TO FINISH: Divide the hot grits among 6 warm bowls. Spoon the shrimp and sausage mixture over the grits. Sprinkle with the remaining parsley and serve immediately.

Chicken Gravy

Makes 4 1/2 cups

4 tablespoons butter

1/2 cup all-purpose flour

1 quart chicken stock (see page 10)

In a heavy-bottomed stockpot, melt the butter and add the flour to make a roux. Cook over very low heat for 3 to 5 minutes, or until it has a nutty aroma. Slowly add the chicken stock, stirring constantly with a whisk. Increase the heat to a high simmer and continue stirring. It's important at this time to get all the lumps out by whisking briskly. Reduce the heat to low and allow the gravy to simmer for 10 minutes to cook out any starchy flavor. Remove from heat and keep warm.

Creamy White Grits

Makes 8 cups

2 quarts water

2 1/2 cups coarse stone-ground white grits

1 cup heavy cream

2 tablespoons butter

1 tablespoon salt

1/4 teaspoon white pepper

In a heavy-bottomed stockpot or large saucepan, bring the water to a boil. Slowly add the grits while continuously stirring. Bring to a boil again, then reduce the heat to low and continue stirring to prevent grits from sticking to the bottom and scorching. After 8 to 10 minutes, the grits will plump up. Continue cooking on low heat for 15 to 20 minutes, stirring frequently. Add the cream, butter, salt and white pepper and continue to cook for an additional 15 minutes. The grits should have a thick, creamy consistency. Keep covered and warm until ready to serve. If they become too thick, add warm water until they are the desired consistency.

Fish, Greens and Grits

Serves 4

SALMON

4 salmon fillets, about 5 ounces each

Salt and ground black pepper

2 tablespoons olive oil

BEURRE BLANC

1/2 cup unsalted butter, cold, divided

2 shallots, finely diced

1 tablespoon dry white wine or Champagne

1/4 cup heavy cream

1 teaspoon lemon zest

1 tablespoon water (if needed)

Pinch of fine sea salt and white pepper

WILTED GREENS

2 tablespoons butter

12 ounces of your favorite greens (e.g., sweet potato leaves, broccoli leaves or spinach)

1 Roma tomato, diced

Fine sea salt and white pepper

GRITS

6 cups water

2 cups coarse stone-ground grits

1/2 cup heavy cream

Salt and white pepper

TO FINISH

4 pieces cooked bacon, crumbled

1 cup crumbled feta cheese

SALMON: Heat the grill or skillet. Season the salmon with salt and pepper and brush the fillets with olive oil. Place fillets skin side up on the hot grill or skillet and cook for 3 minutes per side, or longer for well done. Remove salmon from the grill, plate and keep warm.

BEURRE BLANC: Heat 4 tablespoons of butter, add shallots and cook for 2 to 3 minutes, or until the shallots are soft but not browned. Add the wine, cook for 1 to 2 minutes, add the cream and reduce by one-third, then add the lemon zest. Gradually whisk in the remaining butter a little at a time. If the sauce gets too hot it will separate. When all the butter has been whisked into the sauce, the sauce should coat the back of a spoon. If it's too thick, add a tablespoon of water to thin. Adjust salt and pepper to taste.

WILTED GREENS: Melt butter in a large sauté pan. Add greens and cook over a medium-low heat until just wilted. Add the tomato, cook for 1 minute more, then remove pan from heat and keep warm. Season to taste with salt and pepper.

GRITS: Bring the water to a boil in a heavy-bottomed pan. Slowly pour in the grits, stirring as you go to prevent lumps. Reduce the heat to low and continue stirring to prevent grits from settling on the bottom, about 5 minutes. Cook covered for about 35 to 40 minutes more, stirring frequently. When the grits have absorbed all the liquid and are soft, add the cream and season with salt and pepper to taste. The grits should be thick and creamy. Remove from heat and keep warm.

TO FINISH: Put a generous scoop of grits on each of 4 dinner plates. Lay a piece of cooked salmon just off to the side. Top with a generous serving of wilted greens. Spoon the beurre blanc on top and garnish with chopped bacon and feta cheese.

FISH & SHELLFISH

Campfire-Style Spot Tail Bass

Serves 4

This recipe is an adaptation of one from Magnolias alumni Jeremy Ashby. Also a Johnson & Wales graduate, he has achieved great success in his career, including his current role as executive chef at Brasabana and Azur restaurants in Lexington, Kentucky.

2 pounds spot tail bass, filleted and cut into 4 portions

Spice mix (recipe follows), divided

1 tablespoon olive oil

1/3 pound country ham, diced

2 cloves garlic, thinly sliced

1 medium yellow onion, diced small

1 green bell pepper, diced

1 medium tomato, diced

1 tablespoon hot sauce

2 ears fresh corn, each cut into 4 pieces

3/4 can Pabst Blue Ribbon beer or whatever you drink while fishin'

1 lemon, halved

2 tablespoons butter

Sea salt and ground black pepper

Season the bass with half the spice mixture. In a large cast iron skillet heated over a campfire, add olive oil and the ham. Cook ham until fat is rendered and the ham is golden brown and slightly crispy, about 5 minutes. Add garlic, onion and bell pepper. Sauté until onion is translucent, 3 to 5 minutes. Add tomato, hot sauce and remaining spice mixture to pan and stir. Place ears of corn on one side of the skillet and the bass on the opposite side. Add beer to deglaze pan and then cover to steam for 8 minutes, until the fish has cooked through.

Carefully remove fish from the skillet and divide among serving plates. Squeeze lemon halves over the skillet then remove from heat. Fold in butter and season to taste with salt and pepper. Spoon sauce and corn over the fish fillets and serve.

Spice Mix

Makes 2 tablespoons

2 teaspoons salt

2 teaspoons garlic powder

1 teaspoon oregano

1 teaspoon onion powder

1 teaspoon thyme

Combine all ingredients in a bowl and mix well.

Boiled Peanut–Crusted Tuna with Crispy Broccoli Salad Spring Rolls, Spicy Mustard and Peach Syrup *Makes 8 appetizers or 4 entrées*

This is a really easy dish using store-bought items, or you can make it all from scratch. We always have a good amount of broccoli stalks left over, so one day for the staff meal instead of making broccoli soup, one of the guys made a slaw that turned into a salad and finally evolved to the filling for a rice paper roll. A recipe was born!

TUNA

8 tuna fillets, 3 to 4 ounces each

1/4 cup boiled peanut rub (recipe follows)

2 tablespoons olive oil

Spicy mustard (see page 122)

Broccoli salad spring rolls (see page 122)

Peach syrup (see page 122)

1 cup boiled peanuts (see page 42)

1 1/2 ounces baby cilantro sprouts

Rub the tuna fillets with the boiled peanut rub on all sides. Cover and refrigerate for at least 2 hours or overnight.

TO FINISH: Heat 2 tablespoons of olive oil in a heavy-bottomed sauté pan over medium-high heat. Carefully place the tuna fillets in the heated oil and sear them until medium rare and slightly crusty on the outside, about 2 1/2 minutes on each side. Place 8 plates on the counter and, using a soupspoon, place a dollop of spicy mustard on each plate. Create an artistic bushstroke on the plate by pulling back the spoon, leaving a small trail of mustard. Cut the spring roll in half diagonally and place it off-center on the plate. Cut the tuna into 3 slices and place on top of the spring roll. Drizzle peach syrup around the plate and garnish with boiled peanuts and cilantro.

Boiled Peanut Rub *Makes 3 cups*

1/4 cup coriander seeds

1 cup olive oil

1 1/2 cup boiled peanuts, finely chopped (see page 42)

2 tablespoons freshly ground black pepper

2 tablespoons ground ginger

2 tablespoons coarse sea salt

1/2 teaspoon cayenne pepper

Preheat oven to 375 degrees F.

Place the coriander seeds on a sheet tray in the oven for 4 minutes. When you start to smell them toasting, remove from oven and cool. Use a spice grinder to grind the roasted coriander seeds to a coarse meal (don't grind to a powder). In a small bowl, mix the olive oil, boiled peanuts, black pepper, ginger, salt, cayenne pepper and ground coriander. Mix well to combine.

Broccoli Salad

Makes 1 quart

2 large bunches fresh broccoli

2 carrots, peeled

$1/4$ head red cabbage

1 red bell pepper

OR substitute 2 (12-ounce) bags of pre-chopped broccoli slaw

2 (3-ounce) bags oriental flavor ramen noodles

$1/4$ cup light olive oil

$1/8$ cup boiled peanuts

Salt and pepper

Use a sharp knife to cut broccoli tops from stems and cut into small florets. Peel the stems using a potato peeler or knife. Using a mandolin, julienne the broccoli stems, carrots, cabbage and red pepper. Be careful with the mandolin—it is very sharp. Or skip this step and substitute two bags of precut slaw.

Cook noodles according to directions, drain and reserve the liquid. Let the noodles cool, then chop into 1-inch lengths. Set aside in a medium-sized colander to drain.

Return the noodle liquid to the saucepot and bring to a boil. Quickly blanch the florets, about 3 minutes. Remove from heat and place the broccoli in an ice-water bath to stop cooking; drain and reserve.

In a large sauté pan over medium heat, add the olive oil and sauté all of the julienned vegetables just until wilted. Remove vegetables from heat and add to the noodles, broccoli tops, and boiled peanuts—all in the colander. Press out extra liquid. Season with salt and pepper to taste.

continued >

Spring Rolls

Makes 8 spring rolls

8 rice paper wrappers

Broccoli salad (see page 121)

1 cup of cornstarch for dusting, plus 2 tablespoons for sealing

2 tablespoons cold water

12 cups canola oil for frying

Lay the egg roll wrappers on a clean, dry surface dusted lightly with cornstarch, orienting the wrappers in a diamond shape. Portion $1/2$ cup of the broccoli salad in the center of each wrapper. Place 1 cup cornstarch in a small bowl and slowly whisk in the 2 tablespoons of water to make slurry that is free of lumps. Lightly brush the edges of each rice paper wrapper with the slurry. Fold the bottom quarter of the diamond up toward the top. Fold the two sides inward to form an envelope. Bring the top corner over towards you. Press the edges to seal the rolls. Dust with the cornstarch to keep them dry.

Pour the canola oil into a deep fryer or frying pan with a thermometer and heat the oil to 325 degrees F. Carefully place half of the rolls into the fryer. Cook until golden brown. The rolls will float to the top when done. Remove from fryer and place on paper towels or brown paper bag to absorb excess oil. Repeat with the remaining 4 rolls. Keep warm.

Spicy Mustard

Makes 1 $1/2$ cups

2 tablespoons dry mustard

4 tablespoons water

$1/2$ cup mayonnaise

$3/4$ cup honey

1 tablespoon whole grain mustard

1 $1/2$ teaspoons chopped parsley

Mix the dry mustard and water together to form a smooth paste. Add remaining ingredients, mix well. Store in an airtight container.

Peach Syrup

Makes 1 $1/2$ cups

2 cups fresh or frozen peaches

$1/2$ cup chopped yellow onion

1 tablespoon plus 1 teaspoon peeled and chopped ginger

$1/2$ cup finely chopped red pepper

$1/2$ cup packed brown sugar

$1/2$ cup granulated sugar

2 tablespoons cider vinegar

In a heavy-bottomed saucepan over medium-low heat, combine all ingredients and cook for 30 minutes, stirring occasionally, until the syrup thickens. When thickened, place in a blender or food processor fitted with a metal blade and blend until smooth. Use right away or chill and store in an airtight container.

Roasted Carolina Shrimp with a Garlic, Parmesan and Toasted Herb Crust   *Serves 4 to 6*

This is a great dish to make when guests are coming. It can be served as an appetizer or an entrée. The recipe can be assembled in advance and popped into the oven about the time your guests arrive.

2 pounds large (16–20 count) shrimp, shells on, heads off

3 tablespoons olive oil

2 tablespoons white wine

3 teaspoons coarse sea salt

2 teaspoons ground black pepper

8 tablespoons butter

1/4 cup minced shallots

4 teaspoons minced garlic (4 cloves)

1/4 teaspoon crushed red pepper flakes

2/3 cup panko bread crumbs

2 tablespoons lemon juice, plus 1 tablespoon

1 teaspoon lemon zest

1 cup grated Parmigiano-Reggiano cheese

2 teaspoons chopped fresh thyme

3 tablespoons chopped fresh parsley

1 large cooked egg yolk, grated

Lemon wedges and parsley sprigs for garnish

Preheat the oven to 400 degrees F. Holding a shrimp with the back of the shell cupped in your hand, use scissors to cut the shell toward the tail, but not going all the way. With your thumb and forefinger peel away the shrimp shell, leaving the tail intact. Save shells for later use. Use a knife to remove the vein that runs down the back of the shrimp and discard. Shell all the shrimp in this manner. Place the peeled and deveined shrimp in a large freezer bag with the olive oil, wine, salt and pepper. Let them marinate for 20 to 30 minutes.

In a small saucepan, melt the butter and sauté the shallots, garlic and red pepper flakes about 2 minutes. Remove from heat and set aside.

In a medium-sized bowl add the bread crumbs, 2 tablespoons lemon juice, lemon zest, cheese, thyme, parsley, egg yolk, and the ingredients from the sauté pan. Mix well to combine.

Pour the marinade from the bag of shrimp into a large ovenproof dish and arrange the shrimp, tails standing up, starting from the outside and working toward the middle. Sprinkle the seasoned bread crumb mixture over the shrimp. Roast in the oven until shrimp are pink and the crumbs are toasted, about 10 to 15 minutes. Remove from oven and sprinkle with remaining lemon juice.

Cornmeal-Crusted Blue Ridge Mountain Trout with Shrimp, Local Summer Pea and Bean Succotash, Country Ham and Horseradish Rémoulade

Serves 6

1 cup cornmeal

1 1/2 cups crumbled cornbread (see page 28)

1/2 teaspoon coarse sea salt

1/4 teaspoon ground black pepper

6 trout fillets or 3 whole butterflied trout

1/4 cup canola oil

Shrimp, country ham and local summer pea succotash (recipe follows)

12 ounces tomato butter (see page 45)

Horseradish rémoulade (recipe follows)

In a food processor fitted with a metal blade, add the cornmeal and cooked cornbread, salt, and pepper, and pulse it a few times. Pour into a large baking tray. Dredge the trout fillets in the cornbread mix until well coated.

In a large cast iron skillet, add the canola oil and the cornbread-crusted trout and sauté on medium heat for about 2 1/2 minutes on each side, until nicely light golden brown; keep warm.

If you prefer, you can bake the trout on a sheet tray in the oven at 350 degrees F for 5 to 7 minutes without flipping.

Divide the shrimp and succotash equally among six plates, and place the trout fillets on top. Ladle 2 ounces of tomato butter around the outside of each plate. Using a squirt bottle, zigzag the horseradish rémoulade across the top of the dish. Serve immediately.

Shrimp, Country Ham and Local Summer Pea Succotash

Serves 6

2 teaspoons canola oil

18 (21–25 count) shrimp, or about 3/4 pound

1/2 cup chopped country ham

1 cup sweet corn, cooked

1 cup hominy, cooked

1 cup trinity, cooked (see page 12)

2 cups assorted summer beans and peas, cooked

1 tablespoon chopped parsley

1 tablespoon chopped basil

Coarse sea salt and ground black pepper

In a large skillet over medium-high heat, add the canola oil and sauté the shrimp and country ham for about 4 minutes. Add the sweet corn, hominy, trinity, beans and peas, parsley and basil and cook until the shrimp are done, about 3 minutes. Season to taste with salt and pepper. Keep warm.

Horseradish Rémoulade

Makes 2 cups

1/4 cup prepared horseradish

1 cup mayonnaise

1/2 cup sour cream

2 tablespoons buttermilk

2 tablespoons apple cider vinegar

1 tablespoon Dijon mustard

Pinch of finely minced chives

Place all ingredients in a small bowl and mix well. Store in a squirt bottle or airtight container until ready to use. Will keep for a week refrigerated.

Grilled Snapper with Shrimp, Oyster, and Andouille Sausage Jambalaya, Blackened Tomatoes and Tomato Butter

Serves 6

6 snapper fillets

2 tablespoons olive oil

Sea salt and ground black pepper

Jambalaya (recipe follows)

1 1/2 cups tomato butter (see page 45)

Blackened tomatoes (recipe follows)

Season the fish with olive oil and salt and pepper to taste. Place over hot coals and grill 3 minutes on each side. Remove from heat and keep warm.

TO FINISH: Place 6 dinner plates on the counter. Put a generous scoop of the jambalaya on each plate. Top with a piece of grilled snapper. Drizzle the tomato butter over the fish and place 2 slices of grilled tomato on each plate.

Jambalaya

Serves 6

1/4 cup olive oil

3/4 cup finely chopped tasso ham

2/3 cup chopped Andouille sausage

2 cups finely chopped Vidalia onion

6 green onions, chopped

4 cloves garlic, crushed and minced

1 (3.5-ounce) can chopped green chiles

1 large red bell pepper, diced

6 ribs celery, chopped

8 ripe tomatoes, blanched, peeled, seeded and chopped

3 cups chicken stock, plus more if needed

1 tablespoon chopped fresh oregano

1 tablespoon chopped fresh cilantro

1 teaspoon chopped fresh thyme

3 dried bay leaves

1 teaspoon ground cumin

2 teaspoons chopped fresh basil

3 cups Carolina Plantation rice

24 medium shrimp, peeled and deveined

24 fresh local oysters, about a pint shucked

1/2 pound jumbo lump crabmeat, well picked for shells

Coarse sea salt

Preheat oven to 350 degrees F. In a large skillet heat the olive oil, add the ham and sausage and sauté over medium heat until crispy, about 5 to 7 minutes. Add the Vidalia onion, green onion, garlic, green chiles, bell pepper, celery, tomatoes, 3 cups chicken stock and seasonings. Bring to a boil and stir in the rice. Cover the skillet with a lid or foil and place in the oven for 20 minutes.

Remove from the oven and stir in the seafood. Cover the skillet and return to the oven, cooking an additional 10 minutes. Remove jambalaya from oven and discard the bay leaves. Taste and season with salt if needed.

Blackened Tomatoes

Serves 6

6 Roma tomatoes, halved

3/4 cup Magnolias blackening spice (see page 22)

Rub the tomatoes with blackening spice and grill with the cut side down for 2 minutes; then give each piece a quarter turn and cook for 1 more minute. Remove from heat and keep warm.

Grilled Jumbo Sea Scallops with Lobster and Corn Chowder

Serves 6

GRILLED SCALLOPS

18 U-10 scallops

2 tablespoons olive oil

1 tablespoon finely minced thyme

1 tablespoon finely minced tarragon

Coarse sea salt and ground black pepper

12 skewers soaked in water

TO FINISH

Lobster and corn chowder (recipe follows)

Crumbled reserved bacon

Chopped parsley and chives for garnish

GRILLED SCALLOPS: Heat up the grill. While the grill is getting hot, place the scallops on a shallow plate and drizzle on the olive oil and sprinkle with chopped herbs and salt and pepper to taste. Give each scallop a good coating of seasoning. Let sit for about 15 minutes. Take three scallops and line them in a row and run 2 skewers through the scallops. Place back into the shallow bowl. Repeat with the remaining scallops.

When the grill is hot, make sure the grates are clean. Shake off any excess olive oil and place the scallops on the grill; cook for about 4 minutes on one side to get good grill marks, then turn and cook just until opaque in the middle, about 2 minutes. Use a fish spatula to remove the scallops from the grill. Keep warm.

TO FINISH: Place 6 large dinner bowls on the counter and fill halfway with lobster and corn chowder. Place 3 grilled scallops on top. Garnish with crumbled bacon, parsley and chives.

Lobster and Corn Chowder

Serves 6

POACHING WATER FOR THE LOBSTERS

1 tablespoon olive oil

1 carrot, peeled and diced

1 leek, cleaned and chopped

2 ribs celery, chopped

1 cup white wine

1 gallon water

Bouquet garni of thyme, bay leaf and black peppercorns

3 lobsters, 1 pound each

4 cups fresh corn cut from 8 cobs

8 slices applewood-smoked bacon

$1/2$ cup (1 stick) unsalted butter

$1 1/2$ cups chopped leeks

$3/4$ cup peeled and diced carrots

$1 1/2$ cups chopped celery

$1/2$ cup all-purpose flour

3 cups reserved lobster and corn stock

2 cups milk

2 cups heavy cream

1 cup diced pared parsnips, cooked

2 cups diced pared potatoes, cooked

$1/2$ cup sherry

2 cups chopped lobster meat

Coarse sea salt and ground black pepper

In a large stockpot over medium-high heat, add the olive oil and sauté the carrot, leeks and celery until soft, about 3 minutes. Deglaze the pot with the wine, add the water and bouquet garni and bring to a boil. Add the whole lobsters to the pot and cook for 8 minutes. Reserving the cooking liquid, remove the lobster from the pot and shock under cold water. Remove the meat from the lobsters and place the shells and juices back into the poaching liquid. Simmer the stock on low while you prep the chowder.

After cutting the corn from the cobs, add the cobs to the lobster poaching liquid. Simmer for 30 minutes. Strain and reserve the lobster and corn stock;

discard the solids. Place liquid back into the pot and reduce to 3 cups. Remove from heat and set aside.

In a medium-sized saucepan, fry the bacon until crispy, remove from pan and set aside. Add the butter to the bacon fat and sauté the leeks, carrots and celery until soft. Sprinkle and stir flour into the mixture to make a blond roux, cooking for 3 to 4 minutes. Next add the reserved lobster and corn stock, whisking constantly to remove any lumps. Add the milk and cream. Bring to a low simmer and add the corn, parsnips, potatoes and sherry and cook for 10 minutes. Add the lobster meat then season to taste with salt and pepper. Keep warm.

Pan-Fried Catfish with Carolina Peach Salsa and Blue Crab Hushpuppies

Serves 4

4 (6-ounce) catfish fillets

$1/2$ teaspoon cumin

$1/4$ teaspoon salt

$1/4$ teaspoon freshly ground black pepper

$1/2$ cup cornmeal

$1/4$ cup vegetable oil

Lime wedges

Peach salsa (recipe follows)

Blue crab hushpuppies (recipe follows)

Sprinkle catfish with cumin, salt and pepper. Dredge fillets in cornmeal. In a medium skillet, add oil. Cook catfish on medium-high heat for 3 to 4 minutes on each side, or until fish flakes when tested with a fork.

TO SERVE: Place one fillet on each plate and top with peach salsa. Evenly divide hushpuppies among the plates and scatter around the catfish. Garnish with a lime wedge.

Peach Salsa

Makes 4 cups

12 ripe freestone peaches

$1/4$ cup small-dice red bell pepper

2 tablespoons seeded and finely diced jalapeño

1 lime, juice and zest

2 tablespoons chopped cilantro

$3/4$ teaspoon kosher salt

$1/4$ teaspoon freshly ground black pepper

$3/4$ teaspoon chili powder

2 tablespoons apple cider vinegar

Peel peaches with small paring knife and cut in half around the seed. Pull apart and discard seeds. Cut peaches into $1/2$-inch dice and place

in a large mixing bowl. Combine all ingredients with the peaches and refrigerate until ready to use.

Blue Crab Hushpuppies

Makes approximately 18

4 strips bacon

$1/4$ cup bacon drippings

$1/2$ cup whole milk

4 tablespoons unsalted butter

$1/2$ cup finely diced onion

1 teaspoon onion powder

$1/8$ teaspoon cayenne pepper

$1/2$ teaspoon sugar

1 teaspoon coarse sea salt

$1/2$ cup yellow cornmeal

$3/4$ cup White Lily Self-Rising flour

3 large eggs

1 cup Parmesan cheese

$1/2$ pound jumbo lump blue crabmeat

Oil for frying

Cook bacon in skillet until crispy. Remove from pan and place on a paper towel or brown paper bag, reserving $1/4$ cup of the bacon fat. When bacon has cooled, chop to make $1/2$ cup.

In a medium saucepot add the milk, bacon fat and butter and bring to a high simmer. Add the onion, onion powder, cayenne pepper, sugar and salt. Stir with a solid spoon.

Mix together the cornmeal and flour. Add the flour mixture to the simmering milk and mix well with spoon for about 2 to 3 minutes. Remove from heat and place in the bowl of a stand mixer fitted with a paddle. On medium-low speed, add the eggs one at a time, beating well after each addition. When all eggs are mixed in, pour in the cheese and chopped bacon and mix well. Add the crabmeat and mix very quickly, keeping the lumps whole and intact.

Heat 2 inches of oil in a heavy-bottomed pan to 340 degrees F and, using a small scoop, scoop quarter-size balls into the hot oil about 6 at a time. Cook for about 3 to 4 minutes, or until golden brown. Place on a brown paper bag or paper towel; keep warm until all the hushpuppies have been fried.

Flounder Meunière

Serves 4

This is one of my favorite fish preparations and it's super easy. You can use this recipe with just about any variety of fish. Ask your fishmonger for the top side, or dark side, of the fish. The fillets are meatier.

$3/4$ cup all-purpose flour

3 teaspoons coarse sea salt, divided

2 teaspoons ground black pepper, divided

4 flounder fillets, about 6 to 8 ounces each

6 tablespoons unsalted butter

$1/2$ cup white wine

Juice of 3 lemons

1 teaspoon lemon zest

1 tablespoon capers

1 tablespoon minced parsley

Combine the flour, 2 teaspoons salt and 1 teaspoon pepper in a large disposable freezer bag or brown paper bag. Pat the flounder fillets dry and set aside.

Heat 3 tablespoons butter in a large skillet or sauté pan over medium-high heat. Dredge half of the flounder fillets in the seasoned flour. I like to use the bags so cleanup is easier.

Place the fillets good side down in the pan. Lower the heat to medium and sauté for 2 minutes, turn the fish over and sauté for another 2 minutes. Add half of the wine, juice from 1 lemon, half of the lemon zest and half of the capers to the pan.

While the fish is cooking, spoon the sauce on top of it, coating the fish well. Remove fish from pan and place on a large ovenproof platter to keep warm. Wipe the pan out with a cloth and repeat the process. When all the fish have been cooked, sprinkle with remaining salt, pepper, parsley, capers and lemon juice.

Pan-Fried Soft-Shell Crab, Cornbread Purée, Grilled Green Beans, Southern Chow-Chow, Roasted Corn Sauce

Serves 4

This dish all comes together during the last weeks of soft-shell season. Here in Charleston we're lucky enough to get two crab shedding seasons each year, in the spring and the fall. When crabs shed their skins, the meat and shell are all very tender and edible as a whole. The crab can be used in a variety of ways, from sandwiches to stew. In this recipe it's pan-fried to perfection so the delicate flavor of the crab comes through in each and every bite.

6 jumbo soft-shell crabs, cleaned

$1/2$ cup buttermilk

Canola oil for frying

$1/2$ cup all-purpose flour seasoned with coarse sea salt and freshly ground black pepper

2 cups cornbread purée (recipe follows)

Grilled greens beans (recipe follows)

Roasted corn sauce (recipe follows)

1 cup chow-chow (see page 16)

Clean the crabs and place in a small bowl with buttermilk. Allow to sit for 30 minutes.

In a large skillet, add enough oil to come up a $1/4$ inch along the sides. Heat oil to around 325 degrees F. Remove crabs from the buttermilk and dredge in flour, shaking off any excess. Carefully place in the oil and pan-fry the crabs 3 minutes on each side, or until golden brown, being careful of splattering oil. Remove from pan and place on absorbent paper and keep warm.

TO FINISH: Place 4 rectangular plates on the counter. Spoon 3 small mounds of cornbread purée on each plate in 3 small rows side by side. Top each mound with 2 to 3 green beans. Cut the crabs in half. Place one-half with the cut side down into the cornbread purée. Spoon corn sauce around the crabs, making a figure-eight design. Garnish each crab with chow-chow. Bon appétit!

Cornbread Purée

Makes 3 cups

Make the cornbread a day ahead and cut into cubes. Let dry overnight on a sheet tray.

2 tablespoons bacon drippings

2 cups crumbled cornbread (see page 28)

1 cup buttermilk, plus more as needed

$1/2$ cup shredded smoked Gouda cheese

Coarse sea salt and freshly ground black pepper

In a medium-sized saucepot over medium heat, add the bacon drippings. When hot, add the crumbled cornbread and toast a little more. Add the buttermilk and cheese and simmer over medium heat. Whisk constantly until the mixture reaches a thick, grits-like consistency. Season with salt and pepper to taste. Transfer to a food processor or blender and process until smooth. Add a little buttermilk if needed. Place in a medium bowl and keep warm.

Roasted Corn Sauce

Serves 4

2 ears of corn

$1/2$ cup white wine

2 tablespoons champagne vinegar

2 tablespoons lemon juice

2 stems lemon thyme

$1/2$ bay leaf

$1/2$ teaspoon black peppercorns

$1\,1/2$ cups heavy cream

$1\,1/2$ cups chicken stock

Pull corn husk down. Remove silk and re-wrap husk around corn in its original shape. Roast the corn in a 350-degree oven until kernels just begin to brown. Remove corn from cob. Combine white wine, vinegar, lemon juice, lemon thyme, bay leaf and black peppercorns in a small saucepan over medium heat and reduce to a $1/4$ cup. Add cream and stock and reduce all to $1\,1/2$ cups. Strain the reduction, add corn, and then purée. Strain through a fine mesh strainer. Adjust consistency with more chicken stock if needed.

Grilled Green Beans

Serves 4

$1/2$ pound green beans, blanched

2 cloves garlic, minced

1 tablespoon olive oil

$1/2$ teaspoon red pepper flakes

Salt and ground black pepper

Heat the grill to 350 degrees F. In a medium bowl combine all the above ingredients. Place in a grill basket and grill until soft, about 5 minutes. If you don't have a grill basket, place beans on the top grate, close the lid and cook for 5 to 6 minutes. Keep warm.

Roasted Grouper, Shrimp Scampi Sauce, Roasted Garlic and Parmesan Potatoes, Johns Island Spinach

Serves 4

Grouper works well in many recipes, cooked any style, and it's one of my favorite fish to eat. It has a firm white flesh that holds up well in the frying pan or on the grill. We get a good variety of groupers at the local seafood docks here in Charleston, ranging from black, gray, snowy, yellowedge, red, gags and scamps. Grouper can get quite expensive at certain times of the year, depending on the weather patterns. Feel free to substitute almost any firm, fresh white fish for the grouper.

4 grouper fillets, 5 to 6 ounces each

1 teaspoon coarse sea salt

$1/2$ teaspoon white pepper

2 tablespoons olive oil

Roasted garlic and parmesan potatoes (recipe follows)

Sautéed spinach (recipe follows)

Shrimp scampi sauce (recipe follows)

Preheat oven to 250 degrees F. Season the fish with salt and pepper. Heat an ovenproof skillet large enough to hold the fish over medium-high heat. Add olive oil and heat until hot, then add the fillets and cook until lightly golden on the first side, about 3 minutes. Carefully flip the fish in the pan and place in the oven to finish cooking, about 7 minutes, or just until it's barely opaque throughout. It will continue to cook a little bit off the heat. Keep warm.

TO FINISH: Place 4 warm dinner plates on the counter. Place a large spoonful of the mashed potatoes on each plate and next to them a smaller serving of spinach. Top with a roasted grouper fillet and then the shrimp scampi sauce, dividing the shrimp and sauce equally across the top of the fish. Enjoy.

Roasted Garlic and Parmesan Potatoes

Serves 4

4 baking potatoes, peeled and diced

6 cups cold water

2 tablespoons coarse sea salt, plus 1 teaspoon

1/2 cup milk

4 tablespoons butter

3 tablespoons roasted garlic purée (see page 18)

4 tablespoons grated Parmesan cheese

White pepper

Put the potatoes, water and 2 tablespoons of salt in a saucepan and bring to a boil over medium-high heat. Lower to a simmer and cook for 18 to 20 minutes, or until the potatoes are tender.

Place the milk, butter, garlic purée and Parmesan in a small saucepan and heat until the butter is melted. Reserve and keep warm.

Drain the liquid from the potatoes and return the pot to the burner. Steam dry the potatoes, stirring constantly. Remove from heat and put potatoes through a food mill or potato ricer. Carefully blend the warm Parmesan and roasted garlic cream mixture into the potatoes. Season with remaining salt and white pepper. Use a whisk or mixer with a whip attachment to whip up the potatoes. Serve immediately.

Sautéed Spinach

Serves 4

3 tablespoons butter

1 pound baby spinach leaves, washed and dried

Pinch of coarse sea salt

Pinch of white pepper

Heat butter in a large heavy-bottomed skillet. Add the spinach and cook over medium-low heat until wilted. Season with salt and pepper to taste. Drain and keep warm.

Shrimp Scampi Sauce

Serves 4

2 teaspoons olive oil

1 large shallot, minced

2 tablespoons finely diced tomato

2 cups sliced mushrooms

2 cloves garlic, crushed and minced

16–24 (30-count) shrimp, peeled and deveined

1/2 cup white wine

Juice of 1 lemon

3 tablespoons butter, cut into cubes

1 teaspoon coarse sea salt

1 teaspoon ground black pepper

Heat the olive oil in a heavy-bottomed pan over medium heat. Add the shallots and sauté until soft, about 1 minute. Add the tomato, mushrooms, garlic and shrimp, and sauté for 3 minutes. Add the wine and lemon juice and reduce by two-thirds. Add the butter and melt it one cube at a time. Season with salt and pepper and keep warm.

Parmesan-Crusted Flounder with Jasmine Rice and Creek Shrimp Pirloo with Sweet Corn, Tomato and Asparagus Salad, Citrus Beurre Blanc

Serves 4 for dinner or 6 lunch

This dish has been a customer favorite for many years. When fresh local flounder hasn't been available, I've tried a few times to slip this offering off the menu, but customers raise a fuss and demand that we serve it even if we have to bring the flounder in from elsewhere. I am happy—and flattered—to oblige. There are several steps to the dish, but it's well worth the effort.

2 cups Parmesan crust (recipe follows)

2 1/2 pounds flounder fillets, about 6 ounces per person (check for bones)

4 tablespoons olive oil

Shrimp pirloo (recipe follows)

Carolina jasmine rice (recipe follows)

Sweet corn, tomato and asparagus salad (see page 138)

Citrus berre blanc sauce (see page 138)

1/2 pound jumbo lump crabmeat

Pour the Parmesan crust mixture into a medium-sized bowl and coat the flounder on all sides. Heat a skillet on the stovetop over medium heat (or bake flounder in a 300-degree oven for about 12 to 15 minutes on a sheet tray). Carefully add the olive oil to the pan and place the flounder good side up in the pan. Cook about 2 minutes, turn, and cook for another 3 minutes, or until done. You want a nice golden crust. Keep warm.

Divide the shrimp pirloo among 4 to 6 plates. Place the rice in the center of the plate. Top with the Parmesan flounder. Divide the sweet corn, tomato and asparagus salad evenly on top of the fillets. Ladle the citrus beurre blanc around the outside of the plate. Finish by sprinkling jumbo lump crabmeat on top of the beurre blanc.

Parmesan Crust

Enough for 4 to 6 portions

1 1/4 cup grated Parmesan cheese

3 cups panko bread crumbs

1/4 teaspoon granulated garlic

1/4 teaspoon granulated onion

1 teaspoon paprika

2 tablespoons olive oil

1 tablespoon chopped parsley

Pinch of coarse sea salt and freshly ground black pepper

Measure and place all the ingredients in a food processor fitted with a metal blade. Pulse for 30 seconds. Store in an airtight container.

Shrimp Pirloo

Serves 6

1 tablespoon butter

$^1/_2$ pound shrimp, peeled and deveined (reserve shells for stock)

$^1/_4$ cup diced yellow onion

2 tablespoons diced red bell pepper

1 tablespoons diced cup celery

1 cup lobster stock or shrimp stock (use reserved shells, see page 15)

1 cup heavy cream

3 cups cooked Carolina jasmine rice (see page 138)

$^1/_4$ cup Parmesan cheese

1 teaspoon coarse sea salt

$^1/_2$ teaspoon ground black pepper

$^1/_3$ cup thinly sliced green onion

In a medium-sized skillet over medium-high heat, add the butter and sauté the shrimp, onion, bell pepper and celery. Cook until the shrimp are pink. Add the shellfish stock and heavy cream. Reduce by one-third. Add the rice, cheese, salt, pepper and green onion, and cook until the rice is well coated. Check for seasoning. Remove from heat and serve immediately.

continued >

Carolina Jasmine Rice

Serves 4 to 6

2 cups jasmine rice

3 cups water

1 tablespoon sea salt

Put the rice in a strainer and rinse under cold water to remove some of the unwanted starch.

Place the rice, water and salt in a medium-sized saucepot, cover with a lid and bring slowly to a boil over medium-high heat. When you see steam trying to escape, reduce the heat to low and simmer for about 12 to 15 minutes. It's best not to peek. When the rice is cooked and the lid removed, little steam holes should be present and all water should be absorbed. Let the rice rest for a minute or two, then fluff with a fork.

Sweet Corn, Tomato and Asparagus Salad

Serves 4 to 6

1 tablespoon olive oil or unsalted butter

2 cups ($1/4$-inch pieces) asparagus, blanched (20 spears)

1 cup fresh yellow corn kernels

1 cup cherry tomatoes, halved

2 stems fresh basil, leaves pulled and julienned

$1/2$ teaspoon coarse sea salt

$1/2$ teaspoon freshly ground black pepper

In a medium-sized skillet over medium heat, add the olive oil or the unsalted butter. Add asparagus and sauté for 60 seconds. Add the corn and cook for 30 seconds. Add the cherry tomato halves, basil, salt and pepper, and cook until heated throughout. Keep warm.

Citrus Beurre Blanc

Serves 4 to 6

2 shallots, minced

1 cup dry white wine

2 tablespoons fresh lemon juice

$1/4$ teaspoon black peppercorns

1 bay leaf

$1/2$ cup heavy cream

$1 1/2$ cups unsalted butter, cut into $1/2$-inch pieces

Coarse sea salt and white pepper

Combine the shallots, wine, lemon juice, peppercorns and bay leaf in a nonreactive (non-aluminum) pan over high heat and reduce to 2 tablespoons. Add the cream to the reduction. Let it reduce by two-thirds, or until it starts to bubble. Turn the heat down to low and start adding the butter one piece at a time. (A little trick to help the sauce from breaking: When you whisk in the butter, whisk first piece on the heat and next one off the heat. Continue the rotation until the sauce is fully emulsified.) Remove from heat, strain the sauce through a mesh strainer to remove the spices, and check for seasoning. Keep in a warm place until ready to use.

MEAT & POULTRY

How to Make Your Own Bacon

Serves 8 to 10

There are two ways to cure a pork belly for bacon: dry cure and wet cure. I prefer the wet cure for the most reliable results. Dry curing sometimes produces hot spots or a really salty area due to an excessive amount of spice that wasn't rubbed in or mixed well. In the brine method the belly is submerged, for a more uniform cure. The product gets a better distribution of both brine and spices. For smoking, I like to use a blend of pecan, peach and apple woods.

1 side of pork belly, about 5 pounds (remove skin and save for pork rinds; and trim fat as much as you like)

1/2 cup ground black pepper

1 1/2 tablespoons curing salt (No. 1)*

2 1/2 cups packed brown sugar

1 1/2 cups kosher salt

1/4 cup crushed bay leaves

2 quarts water

2 quarts apple cider

Place the trimmed belly on the counter and press the black pepper and curing salt into the pork belly. In a medium pot, combine remaining ingredients and bring to a simmer until the sugar has melted. Remove from heat and allow to cool. Once the brine is cooled, place the pork belly in a container and pour the brine over the belly, making sure it's completely submerged. Refrigerate for 3 days. Flip the belly and let it sit 2 more days. (I put a weight on mine to make sure it stays submerged.) Remove from brine, pat dry and smoke over a low heat of 165 degrees F for about 15 hours, until tender and the meat reaches an internal temperature of 165 degrees F. The bacon slices more easily and uniformly if well chilled.

*It will be pink, and available in different sizes.

Pork Belly—Have We Had Enough Yet?

Serves 8 to 10

I know! Everywhere you look, pork belly is on the menu. Against my better judgment I'm going to show you how to make your own. I learned from the master himself, Chef Craig Deihl, King of Pork. Real ham enthusiasts try to buy the ham from the left side of the animal. Old-timers insist the left side is tenderer than the right because the hogs like to scratch themselves against the pen post, mostly on the right side, making it tougher.

To figure out whether the pork belly has skin off or on, here's a rule of thumb: If you can put your thumbnail through the top white part of the belly, the skin is off. If not, just remove the skin by peeling it off with a knife, like filleting a fish. Save the skin for cracklings.

5 pounds pork belly	2 ribs celery, chopped
$1/2$ cup kosher salt	2 carrots, chopped
$1/4$ cup white pepper	2 cups red wine
$1/4$ cup chopped fresh sage	$1/3$ cup canola oil
$1/4$ cup chopped fresh thyme	$1/3$ cup butter
$1/3$ cup crushed and chopped garlic	Maple syrup, honey or whiskey (optional)
2 onions, chopped	

Using a sharp knife, trim some of the excess fat from the pork belly, then score the belly skin in a checkerboard fashion. Rub the belly on both sides with salt, pepper, sage, thyme and garlic until evenly coated. Wrap the pork belly in plastic and refrigerate overnight.

Preheat oven to 275 degrees F. Remove pork from wrap and place in a roasting pan, skin side up, on top of the chopped vegetables and red wine. Bake for 3 hours. Turn the oven to broil and cook for 9 to 10 minutes, or until the skin puffs up evenly. Remove from heat and allow to rest.

Using a serrated knife, cut the belly into 3-inch blocks. In a hot sauté pan over medium-high heat, add the oil and pork belly and sear on all sides. Reduce the heat and baste the pork belly with butter, turning it over in the pan and continuing to baste. If you want to dress up the flavor, now is the time to add a good splash of maple syrup, flavored honey, or whiskey to glaze.

How to Make Cracklings and Pork Rinds

Snacks for 8 to 10

People often confuse cracklings and pork rinds and use the terms interchangeably. Though similar, they are two different things. Cracklings are the pork belly skin with a layer of fat still attached. Pork rinds are made using just the skin alone.

4 pounds of pork skin and meat for cracklings (just skin for rinds), cut into squares

5 to 6 cups water

2 tablespoon sea salt

2 cups lard or vegetable oil

CRACKLINGS: First, if there is hair on the skin, use a butane lighter to burn it off. The hair burning produces a very bad smell, so take care of this step outdoors, or simply shave the skin with a hand-held razor.

Using the skin and trim from pork bellies, cut into $3/4$-inch cubes. It's easier to cut when cold, and scissors work best to cut through the skin. When I watched cracklings being cooked at a place outside Lake Charles, Louisiana, the folks there cut the pork, cooked it down in water to soften the outside skin and render the fat, and then deep-fried it.

Into a large pot pour about 2 inches of water and boil the pork to break down the outside skin and render the fat. The water will evaporate and be replaced by the fat from the pork bellies.

Keep a lid on it because it will pop a little. When you hear the popping stop, remove the lid. The cracklings should be nice and golden brown. Remove from heat and place the cracklings onto a brown bag. Raise the heat on the pan to 375 degrees F and add a few pieces at a time; fry until crispy. Season with your favorite spice and serve right away.

PORK RINDS: Wash the pork skin and make sure it's hair free. Cut into 1-inch cubes, place in a pot of water and boil for around 45 minutes. Remove from pan and pat dry. Place in a warm oven (180 degrees F) for about 3 hours to bake and dry. Remove baked rinds from oven. Heat oil in a shallow pan and deep-fry the pork rinds until crunchy. Season with salt and pepper while warm.

I asked my good friend and Magnolias alumni Jeff Delmastro to write the recipes for barbecue (pages 144–146). Jeff is the foremost barbecue expert that I know. He started Mac's Speed Shop barbecue in 2005 in North Carolina. He has five or six locations now and a couple of big rigs for when he hits the road to compete in major barbecue cook-offs around the country. Jeff and his award-winning team have a trophy case that rivals Richard Petty's. Next time you're up in Charlotte, stop by and say hello.

"The key to a great smoked barbecue pulled pork is to start with a good cooking vessel. I've traveled all over the country eating barbecue in some of the best joints in the world. The common denominator always goes back to cooking over real wood and wood chips native to the region. Second, the meat has to be cooked at a very low temperature for a very long time. At Mac's we use woods such as hickory and cherry with some occasional peach. Different regions use woods common to their terrain, sometimes oak or apple. In the Deep South near Texas and the Southwest, folks use mesquite and post oak. But keep in mind that mesquite and post oak are intensely strong smoking flavors that I would recommend only for beef. It tends to overpower pork because it takes on too much of the smoky flavor of the wood. I typically count on a cook time of 1 to 1 1/2 hours per pound of meat, smoking it at 225 to 250 degrees F." —*Jeff Delmastro*

St. Louis Ribs

Serves 4 to 6

2 racks pork ribs	3 cups barbecue dry rub (see page 21)

Using the barbecue dry rub (see page 21), lightly coat both sides of the ribs with rub and allow to sit overnight.

Using the same style smoker as for the butt, smoke the ribs for 3 hours at 250 degrees F.

Remove from the smoker and wrap the ribs in foil, adding a touch of your favorite beer under the ribs, and wrap tightly. Smoke for 1 more hour and remove. You'll know the ribs are done if the meat has pulled away from the bone. Also bend the rib far enough to determine if it will break apart with relative ease. Allow to cool.

Fire up your favorite grill, charcoal or otherwise. Reheat the ribs, basting with your favorite barbecue sauce. It's important to get the sauce to caramelize on the ribs, giving them a slight char. Cut and serve.

Barbecue Pork Butt

Serves 8 to 10

12–14 pound bone-in Boston butt

Barbecue dry rub (see page 21)

Prepare the butt by trimming excess fat, any veins, connective tissue or cartilage on the outside of the meat that doesn't look appetizing or appealing. Generously coat the butt with dry rub and let stand refrigerated for 12 hours.

Choose the proper wood and prepare your smoker by preheating with wood to 225 degrees F. I don't recommend it, but you can also cook the butt in a standard household oven at 225. If you choose the oven route, the meat cooks fine but never achieves the wonderful smoky flavor of genuine barbecue.

Another option: You can inject Boston butt with any of your favorite flavorings or marinades prior to smoking. I recommend keeping it simple. Try not to over-complicate the injection by using flavorings that are too fussy. Your goal is to enhance the flavor of the meat, not smother it. You can inject anywhere from a pint to quart of liquid into a single 12- to 14-pound pork butt. The injection recipe is below.

Place butt in the smoker with the fat cap facing down. Smoke until the meat reaches an internal temperature of 195 to 200 degrees F, or until the bone feels like it's ready to pull out with very little effort. Pull the butt from the smoker and allow to rest for at least 30 to 45 minutes covered with foil. Remove the foil and pull the pork into bite-size chunks, discarding any fat or connective tissue that remains. Most barbecue aficionados say that a good barbecue doesn't need sauce, but if you want to try one, start with a classic South Carolina mustard sauce (see page 24).

Simple Injection Method

1 quart apple juice

1 quart apple cider vinegar

2 cups salt

Combine all ingredients and whisk until the salt dissolves. Inject as much into the pork butt as it will hold. Avoid sticking the injector into the meat too many times. Too much piercing allows the injection and meat juices to seep out. Pick 3 to 4 different spots on the meat to inject and keep injecting those sites until the liquid just begins to seep back into the injector.

Roasted or Grilled Beef Tenderloin   *Serves 10 to 14*

If you buy beef in larger cuts, like a whole beef tenderloin, New York strip or rib-eye, you can lower your cost on steak compared to buying individual ones. Plus you can have the steaks cut to sizes of your choice. Just ask the butcher. I serve this dish with crispy French fries, toasted Brussels sprouts with bacon and cheddar cheese with a shiitake mushroom and truffle veal demi-glace. It's our version of an uptown Philly cheese steak. I like to sear the outside of the meat first then cook it at a lower temperature for the final minutes.

1 (4-to-6-pound) beef tenderloin, trimmed and cleaned

2 tablespoons chopped fresh rosemary

2 tablespoons chopped fresh thyme

3 tablespoons olive oil

2 tablespoons coarse sea salt

2 teaspoons ground black pepper

3 cloves garlic, crushed and chopped

Heat the oven to 450 degrees F. About 1 $1/2$ hours before cooking the tenderloin, remove it from the refrigerator and bring it to room temperature.

In a small bowl add the chopped herbs, olive oil, salt, pepper and garlic. Mix well. Rub this mixture into the meat, coating well. Place the tenderloin in the hot oven or grill and sear the outside until it's a nice brown color, about 12 to 15 minutes. Remove the pan from the oven and turn the temperature down to 300 degrees F. Return the pan to the oven and cook until the meat reaches an internal temperature of 125 degrees F, about 12 to 15 minutes more. If using a grill, place the meat on the top rack, away from the heat, and cook until it reaches 125 degrees F on a digital meat thermometer. Remove from the heat and loosely tent with foil to rest about 15 minutes.

Chicken and Dumplings

Serves 4

1 cup diced potatoes

2 carrots, diced

1 1/2 cups diced onion

2 tablespoons butter

1 tablespoon olive oil

2 bay leaves

1 teaspoon poultry seasoning

2 teaspoons minced fresh thyme

3 tablespoons flour

2 quarts chicken broth

1 1/2 pounds cooked chicken, diced or shredded

1 cup green peas

Dumplings (recipe below)

Salt and ground black pepper

In a medium stockpot or Dutch oven over medium heat, sauté the potatoes, carrots and onions in the butter and olive oil about 5 minutes. Season the mixture with bay leaf, poultry seasoning and thyme. Add the flour to the pan and cook about 2 minutes. Slowly add the chicken broth to the flour, whisking it in until smooth. Cook for 10 minutes and add chicken meat. Return the stew to a simmer, and add peas.

Using a soupspoon, scoop quarter-size dumplings and drop them into the stew, spaced about 1/4 inch apart. You should have about 48 dumplings. Reduce heat to low, cover with a lid and cook for 15 minutes. The dumplings will grow in size. Season to taste with salt and pepper. Serve hot.

Dumplings

Makes 48 dumplings

3 3/4 cups all-purpose flour

1 teaspoon baking powder

1 teaspoon sea salt

2 teaspoons freshly ground black pepper

9 tablespoons butter

6 tablespoons shortening

3 cups heavy cream

In a medium-sized bowl, stir together the flour, baking powder, salt and pepper. Add the butter and shortening and cut into pea-sized pieces. Add the heavy cream and incorporate just until mixed. Turn the dough onto a floured board, knead lightly once or twice, and roll out to 1/2 inch thick. Punch out little rounds of dough about the size of a quarter. Set aside. You will have a little extra dough leftover.

CHICKEN LIVERS, GIZZARDS, CHITLINS, HOG MAW AND TURKEY WINGS

Most of the time our guests never get to try some of the dishes made from the by-products that we use. Some would turn up their noses at the very idea of eating many of them, whether stuffed pig stomachs (hog maws) or the chitlins (pig intestines) with hot sauce, livers and country ham, pressure-cooked chicken gizzards or braised turkey wings with cabbage. These dishes are old-school southern and take a lot of work and time to get right. But follow these recipes and at least you can say you have tried them just once. I'll give you a quick walk-through on how to fix a family-style version of each.

PAN-FRIED CHICKEN LIVERS

Soak the chicken livers in milk for a couple of hours, allowing about 5 to 6 livers per person. Heat a skillet with $1/2$ inch of oil. Lightly coat the livers in seasoned flour and pan-fry until crispy. Put a cover or screen on the pan (be careful, the livers will pop) and cook for about 5 minutes, or until lightly browned. Remove livers from pan and drain on a brown paper bag or paper towels. Keep warm.

In the pan used to cook the livers, add thin slices of country ham and julienned Vidalia onions and sauté until the onions have caramelized. Deglaze the pan with chicken stock and a little coffee. Place a pile of the country ham and onions in the center of each plate, surround it with chicken livers and drizzle the gravy around the plate. Season with salt and pepper.

CHICKEN GIZZARDS

A pressure cooker works best and is the fastest way. Clean and pick through a pound of gizzards and place in the pressure cooker or pot. If using the pressure cooker, add 1 cup of water and cook for 15 minutes, then allow to cool.

If using a pot, place the gizzards in a pot covered with water and a pinch of salt, add a slice of onion and cook at a high simmer for about 50 minutes. Check for tenderness. If gizzards are still tough, cook for another 15 minutes and allow to cool. This can be done a day ahead.

Mix up a batch of seasoned flour, using half panko bread crumbs and half all-purpose flour and a good amount of Creole Seasoning (see page 23). Heat a skillet filled with about an inch of oil, and fry the gizzards in batches. When done, drain on a brown paper bag. Ms. Marshall makes sage pan gravy by draining off all but 2 tablespoons of oil and adding a little flour to make her roux, followed with some sage, salt, pepper and milk until it's creamy. She serves it with white rice and lima beans. But for an appetizer, just serve them with a little dipping sauce.

CHITLINS

Oh, that smell. You must thoroughly wash out the intestines and when you think they're clean and ready, wash them one more time. In this part of the South, hog maw and chitlins are usually served around New Year's. Chitlins cook down a lot and give off a lot of water during the cooking process, so make sure you leave some room in the pot for the extra liquid. A 5-pound tub of raw chitlins will usually yield around 2 1/2 pounds when cooked. Cut chitlins into 7-inch lengths. Wash them very well several times. You should be able to see through them. Place the chitlins in a pot cover with water and par boil twice, draining the water each time. The third time, cover with 3 to 4 cups of chicken stock and 1/4 cup white vinegar. Add half an onion, a bay leaf, crushed red pepper flakes, salt and pepper and simmer for 6 hours, or until tender. Serve with hot sauce.

Big C, our butcher, is from Aiken, South Carolina, a stone's throw from the community of Salley, where they hold the world's largest annual chitlin strut, featuring a hog-calling contest and lots of old-timey southern foods. Big C cooks his chitlins as described here, and then will pan-fry them like pork rinds and dip them in hot sauce. He has worked at Magnolias for over 20 years.

HOG MAWS

Also known as pig stomach, hog maw can be hard to find, but usually a country butcher will have a few. Hog maw is a little chewy and a lot of locals cook it the same way as chitlins, often mixing them together in the same recipe.

Another way is to stuff and roast it. Wash the pork stomach thoroughly with cold water, turning it inside out to make sure it's well cleaned. Sprinkle the stomach with coarse sea salt and scrub the inside and outside of the stomach. Carefully use a sharp knife to cut off any fat you find, and scrape the sides with a sharp knife to remove the thin membrane. Turn the stomach inside out again and rub with a cornstarch and oil mixture, then scrub and rinse again. Quickly blanch the stomach for about 15 seconds. Let cool and rinse again. Pat dry.

Stuff the stomach with the filling of your choice. Here's a great filling combo: Cut up some cabbage, apples and pork sausage, or use turkey wing meat or pork neck meat, and add your choice of spices and herbs. Use any ingredients you'd use when you stuff a Thanksgiving turkey or pork roast. Sew shut the end of the stomach or close it with a skewer. Place some cabbage and bacon in a roasting pan with the maw on top and cook covered for 50 minutes. Add stock as necessary. Slice into 1 1/2-inch-thick portions.

TURKEY WINGS

Clip off the tips of the wings at the first joint. Rinse well and pat dry. Coat the turkey wings with olive oil, poultry seasoning, cayenne, salt and black pepper and braise in a large pan until golden brown. Remove from heat, and add a little flour to the turkey fat in the pan to make a light roux. Stirring constantly, add turkey or chicken broth until the roux and stock produce a creamy gravy. Add a couple slices of onions and green pepper, and return the turkey wings back to the gravy. Cover and cook for an additional 60 minutes. Check for seasoning.

Fried Chicken

Serves 6 to 8

Family traditions run deep in the South. Good, honest fried chicken is one of them, and good fried chicken is difficult to cook at a busy restaurant because it takes a while to cook. But if you love fried chicken the way I do, you'll understand that it's worth the wait. In my family, fried chicken was Sunday supper. That included mashed potatoes, biscuits and gravy. Side dishes would come and go depending on the season, but the rest always stayed the same. Our house is equally divided between the white and dark meat lovers. We still have to cook two chickens to feed the four of us. Some home cooks I know like to use deep-fat fryers, and some won't even cook fried chicken unless they can use a heavy cast iron skillet, preferably one that's been handed down a generation or two. My mom used to have an electric skillet that had two prongs: you plugged a black cloth cord into the pan. It had an adjustable thermostat on the cord and a semi-square-shaped lid . . . I wonder whatever happened to it. Is a lid critical when cooking fried chicken to get that golden crispy texture? Mom said yes. She would cook the chicken for about 30 minutes at 3 different temperatures. First she would begin by frying the chicken on high heat for about 5 minutes. Then she would slow-fry with the lid on, and finish by removing the lid for the last couple of minutes to crisp the chicken. She strained off most of the grease then made her whitewash milk gravy in the skillet. It seems like only yesterday that mom was in the kitchen frying up a batch of Sunday chicken and it sure tasted good.

Lard or peanut or safflower oil

2 kosher or air-chilled chickens, about 3–3 $^1/_2$ pounds, cut up

1 cup Texas Pete hot sauce

2 cups buttermilk

6 cups White Lily Self-Rising flour

2 tablespoons coarse sea salt

1 teaspoon garlic powder

2 teaspoons ground black pepper

1 teaspoon cayenne pepper

$^1/_2$ teaspoon white pepper

Fill a large skillet about half full with lard, peanut oil or safflower oil. I like lard the best.

In a large ziplock bag or container, add the cold chicken and cover with Texas Pete and buttermilk and allow to sit overnight, or a few hours at minimum. In a shallow pan or brown paper bag, add the flour and the seasonings, mixing well. Remove cold chicken from buttermilk a piece at a time and place in the bag. Shake the bag to coat the chicken well, remove, and shake off any excess flour.

Heat the oil on high and add the chicken skin side down. If you're frying different-sized pieces, add the bigger ones first. Fried chicken is best started on high heat, because the temperature of the oil will drop as cold pieces of chicken are added to the pan. When the skillet is full, turn the heat to medium and fry the chicken until just golden brown and crispy, then turn and fry the other side until just golden and crispy.

Turn the skillet down to low, cover and cook for about 10 to 20 minutes, depending on the size of the pieces, and check to make sure it's not cooking too fast or at too high a temperature. Remove the lid and turn the chicken again, turning up the heat enough to crisp up the chicken, but being careful that the oil doesn't get too hot. Keep an eye on it and give it a final turn to crisp the other side. Remove from skillet and keep warm. Let the chicken rest for a while so the juices return into the meat. Serve with your favorite sides.

Southern-Fried Pork Chops With Tasso Ham and Vidalia Onion Brown Gravy

Serves 6

Oil for deep-frying

6 (10-ounce) bone-in pork chops

3 cups buttermilk

1 teaspoon kosher salt

1 teaspoon ground black pepper

1 teaspoon garlic powder

1 teaspoon smoked paprika

1 teaspoon chili powder

3 cups all-purpose flour

When ready to cook, heat oil for deep-frying to 375 degrees F.

Carefully butterfly each pork chop towards the bone. In a large mixing bowl, coat with the buttermilk, making sure each chop is well coated.

Combine salt, pepper, garlic powder, paprika, chili powder and flour. Dredge pork chops in seasoned flour, shaking off the excess flour, and deep fry for approximately 5 to 6 minutes. Season with additional salt and pepper if necessary.

Tasso Ham and Vidalia Onion Brown Gravy

Makes 1 quart

1/4 cup canola oil

1 cup julienned tasso ham

1 cup diced Vidalia onion

1 teaspoon chopped garlic

3 tablespoons all-purpose flour

1 cup red wine

4 cups veal or beef stock, hot

Kosher salt and freshly ground black pepper

Add canola oil and tasso ham to a medium-sized saucepan on medium heat and render the ham until caramelization begins. Next, add the onion and garlic to the rendered tasso and continue cooking until onion is caramelized. Add flour to the rendered mixture and continue cooking for an additional 3 minutes, or until flour begins to lightly brown, stirring continuously. Deglaze with red wine, then add 4 cups of hot veal or beef stock. Lightly simmer for 25 minutes.

You may want to use a hand mixer or blender to blend the gravy until smooth and silky. Season with salt and pepper to taste.

Southern Carpetbagger, Smoked Blue Cheese Béarnaise, Roasted Mushroom and Potato Hash with Madeira Pan Sauce

Serves 4

4 (12-ounce) New York strip steaks

2 tablespoons olive oil

2 tablespoons steak seasoning (see page 21, optional)

Salt and ground black pepper

TO FINISH

Roasted mushroom and potato hash (recipe follows)

1/4 cup crumbled smoked blue cheese or Gouda

Fried oysters (recipe follows)

Pan sauce (recipe follows)

Smoked blue cheese béarnaise (see page 157)

Preheat the oven to 400 degrees F. Rub the steaks with the olive oil and sprinkle with steak seasoning or just salt and pepper. In a large cast iron skillet over high heat, sear the steaks on both sides, about 4 minutes per side. Place the pan in the oven and cook 2 minutes for medium rare, 4 minutes for medium and 6 to 7 minutes for well done. Remove pan from oven and place steaks on a warm plate to rest.

Place four plates on the counter. Equally divide the roasted mushroom and potato hash among them, and using a sharp knife slice a pocket in the side of steak. Fold the steak back and sprinkle the pocket with a fourth of the cheese and stuff with 3 fried oysters. Place the steak on the mushroom and potato hash and ladle the pan sauce over the steak. Finish with a ladle of béarnaise and remaining fried oysters.

Roasted Mushroom and Potato Hash

Serves 4

3 quarts water

1 sweet potato, peeled and cut into 1/2-inch dice

1 pound Yukon Gold potatoes, peeled and diced

1/2 cup chopped red onion

1/4 cup chopped fresh sage

1 pound assorted mushrooms, diced into 1/2-inch pieces

1/2 cup olive oil

1/2 cup chopped and cooked bacon

2 cloves garlic, minced

2 tablespoons butter

Coarse sea salt and freshly ground pepper

Preheat the oven to 400 degrees F and heat a sheet tray in the oven.

In a medium-sized pot add the water and bring to a boil. Add diced potatoes, turn off the heat and let sit for 5 minutes; then drain the potatoes.

In a large bowl add drained potatoes, onion, sage, mushrooms, olive oil, bacon, garlic, and butter; season with salt and pepper to taste. Remove sheet tray from oven, place mixture on the tray and roast for 15 minutes, occasionally turn the mixture on the tray as it roasts. Remove from heat and keep warm.

Fried Oysters

Makes 28 oysters

2 cups buttermilk

2 cups seasoned flour

1 cup cornmeal

3 cups safflower oil

1 pint or 28 oysters

Coarse sea salt and ground black pepper as needed

Using two medium-sized bowls or two large freezer bags, place the buttermilk in one and the seasoned flour and cornmeal in the other.

Heat the oil in a medium-sized saucepot or deep-fat fryer to 350 degrees F.

Drain the oysters and check for shells and particles. Place oysters in the buttermilk and transfer one by one to the flour and cornmeal mixture, evenly coating the oysters. Place on a sheet tray or paper bag. Carefully add the oysters to the hot oil, one or two at a time, and fry until golden brown, about 3 to 4 minutes. Remove from fryer and place on an absorbent cloth or brown paper bag to drain. Season with salt and pepper to taste. Keep warm.

Madeira Pan Sauce

Makes 1 cup

1 shallot, minced

3/4 cup red wine

3/4 cup Madeira wine

Pinch of chopped fresh rosemary

Pinch of chopped fresh thyme

4 tablespoons butter

Salt and freshly ground black pepper (optional)

Add the shallots to the pan used for the steaks and sauté until translucent, about 2 to 3 minutes. Deglaze the pan with red wine and reduce by two-thirds. Add the Madeira and reduce by half; then add the chopped herbs and pour any drippings on the plate into the pan. Whisk in the butter; season with salt and pepper if needed.

continued >

Smoked Blue Cheese Béarnaise

Makes 1 1/2 cups

Use a good smoked blue cheese or substitute smoked Gouda.

1 cup unsalted butter, melted and clarified	1 bay leaf
1/4 cup finely chopped shallots	1/2 teaspoon black peppercorns
2 tablespoons chopped tarragon	3 egg yolks
1/4 cup tarragon vinegar	1/4 cup crumbled smoked blue cheese
1/4 cup white wine	Coarse sea salt and cracked black pepper

To clarify the butter, melt it over low heat and do not stir (stirring causes solids to separate). Remove from heat and skim the solids floating on top. Keep warm.

In a medium-sized saucepot over medium heat, add the shallots, tarragon, vinegar, wine, bay leaf and peppercorns and boil for 5 minutes. You should end up with about 3 tablespoons of the reduction. Strain through a strainer and set off to the side.

Using the double-boiler method, place a pot of water on the stove, and allow to bubble at a high simmer. In a Pyrex or stainless steel bowl, mix the egg yolks and vinegar reduction and place over the hot water bath; slowly stream in a third of the clarified butter, whipping constantly. If it starts to get too hot, remove from hot water for a second, return to the heat and slowly whisk in the remaining butter. Remove from water, add the cheese, and season with salt and pepper. (If using a blender, pour the egg yolks and vinegar reduction in and blend. With the blender running, slowly stream in the clarified butter. Once it emulsifies turn the blender on high and add remaining butter, cheese, and check for seasoning.) Keep warm.

Thanksgiving Day at Magnolias

Serves 12 to 14

Thanksgiving is a busy day at Magnolias—serving around 900 people. We brine 65 turkeys overnight and cooked them the next day. To keep the birds moist, I rub turkey butter under the skin and baste the turkeys with the butter about every 25 minutes. I separate the legs from the breast and cook them at different temperatures and times. The breast is cooked at 200 F and the legs at 325 F with internal temperatures reaching 165 F and 195 F, respectively.

Brined Turkey

2 cups brown sugar

2 cups coarse sea salt

1 bunch thyme

3 bay leaves

2 tablespoons black peppercorns

18–20 pound turkey, giblets and neck removed

2 carrots, peeled and chopped

1 yellow onion, chopped

2 ribs celery, chopped

6 cloves garlic, smashed

Sage butter (recipe follows)

For the turkey brine, bring 1 1/2 gallons of water to boil in a stockpot and add the brown sugar, salt, thyme, bay leaves and peppercorns. Stir until the sugar and salt dissolve. Remove from heat and add 1 gallon of cold water or ice. Allow the brine to come to room temperature. Submerge the turkey in the brine and let sit overnight in the refrigerator or a cool place for 12 to 24 hours. Remove turkey from brine, rinse well and pat dry.

Preheat the oven to 325 degrees F. Scatter the carrots, onion, celery and garlic in the bottom of a heavy-duty roasting pan and add 3 cups of water. Set a roasting rack in the pan. Take a good handful of the sage butter and rub it under the turkey skin and all over the outside of the bird. Spoon the stuffing into the cavity and tie the legs together with kitchen twine. If the bird is already trussed, skip this step. Set the turkey on the rack with the vegetables and roast in the oven, basting with the pan drippings every 25 minutes, until the thigh juice runs clear and the internal temperature of the stuffing reaches 165 degrees F, about 3 1/2 hours. Transfer the turkey to a carving board and cover loosely with foil. Let the bird rest about 20 minutes before carving.

Sage Butter

Makes 3 cups

1 pound unsalted butter, cubed

1 1/2 cups turkey or duck fat

1 bunch sage, chopped

3 cloves garlic, crushed and minced

1 tablespoon coarse sea salt

2 teaspoons white pepper

Using a stand mixer, whip the butter with a paddle attachment until soft, about 3 minutes, then slowly add the fat, sage, garlic, salt and pepper, mixing well. Refrigerate. The butter can prepared and stored up to a week ahead of time.

continued >

Stuffing

Serves 12 to 14

6 tablespoons butter

1 pound Italian sausage, casing removed

2 large yellow onions, diced

2 ribs celery, diced

2 cloves garlic, minced

4 cups chicken stock, plus more if needed (see page 10)

1 large bag stuffing, or 10 cups cubed day-old bread

1 teaspoon thyme

1 tablespoon poultry seasoning

1 teaspoon coarse sea salt

Ground black pepper

1 cup dried cranberries

1 cup diced Granny Smith apples

Melt the butter in a large heavy-bottomed pan and sauté the sausage, breaking it up with a wooden spoon. Cook until most of the pink is gone, then add the onion, celery and garlic and cook until soft. Pour in three-fourths of the chicken stock and bring to a boil, then add dried bread crumbs. Cook until well mixed and the bread is soft, adding more chicken stock if needed. Add the herbs, salt, pepper to taste, cranberries and apples. Check for seasoning and remove from heat. The stuffing can be made a day ahead of time and kept in the refrigerator, but bring it to room temperature before stuffing the bird.

Giblet Gravy

Makes 2 cups

1 onion, chopped

1 rib celery, chopped

Giblets from turkey heart, neck, gizzards, liver

Pan drippings from turkey or unsalted butter

$1/2$ cup all-purpose flour

Salt and ground black pepper

Place the onion, celery and giblets in a pot of cold water (about 6 or 7 cups) and bring to a boil. Reduce to a simmer and cook uncovered for 90 minutes. Strain the stock through a fine sieve, reserving the stock and giblets. In a food processor, quickly chop up the giblets and set aside.

Tilt the roasting pan and remove the vegetables and skim off the fat, measuring out $1/2$ cup of fat. Use the fat and $1/2$ cup flour to make a roux in a small saucepan, cooking about 5 minutes to a light, nutty color and flavor, and remove from heat.

Place the roasting pan across two burners over medium heat and stir the reserved stock into the drippings, scraping up all the brown bits. Slowly add the roux to the pan, whisking constantly to prevent lumps. Reduce heat and simmer to desired thickness. Pass the gravy through a strainer, add the chopped giblets, and season with salt and pepper to taste.

SIDES

BBQ Peanuts

Serves 10 to 12

They're great with grilled pork, as a side dish with barbecue and even as a hot dog topping. Pass the peanuts!

BOILED PEANUTS

3 pounds raw shelled peanuts

2 gallons water to cover

3 tablespoons kosher salt

1 pound bacon, diced

2 onions, diced

$1/2$ cup prepared yellow mustard

$3/4$ cup brown sugar

1 cup ketchup

3 tablespoons lemon juice

$3/4$ cup maple syrup

$1/4$ cup apple cider vinegar

3 pounds cooked peanuts

2 cups peanut potlikker

BOILED PEANUTS: Cover peanuts in water and soak overnight. Drain in the morning.

Add peanuts, water and salt in a large pot and bring to a boil. Cook until the peanuts are softened, about 3 hours. Add more water as needed. Drain the peanuts and reserve 2 cups of the liquid. Makes $1/2$ gallon.

Preheat oven to 350 degrees F.

In a large heavy-bottomed pot over medium heat, render the bacon and pour off half the fat. Add the onions and cook until translucent. Add remaining ingredients except the peanuts and likker, and bring to a simmer. Add cooked peanuts and the peanut likker, and stir. Pour the peanuts into a large ovenproof dish. Wrap with foil and bake for 1 hour. Serve family style.

New Potatoes and String Beans

Serves 6

5 cups snapped, tipped and tailed fresh string beans

5 slices applewood-smoked bacon

2 cups chopped yellow onion

16 very small new potatoes, scrubbed

7 cups water

Coarse sea salt and ground black pepper

Wash beans and set aside. In a heavy-bottomed pan, fry the bacon over low heat until crispy. Add the onion and beans and cook on low for another 10 minutes, stirring until the beans are bright green. Add the potatoes and water and simmer on low heat for 90 minutes. Remove vegetables from the liquid using a slotted spoon. Season to taste with salt and pepper and serve warm.

Brussels Sprouts with Lemon Pangritata

Serves 6 to 8

When buying Brussels sprouts look for tight, green little ones for this recipe.

1/4 cup olive oil, plus 2 tablespoons, divided

1 clove garlic, minced

1 teaspoon freshly grated lemon zest, plus 1 tablespoon, divided

Small pinch of red chile flakes

1 cup bread crumbs

Sea salt and ground black pepper

2 pounds Brussels sprouts

2 tablespoons melted butter

Preheat oven to 375 degrees F.

To make the pangritata, place 1/4 cup olive oil in a heavy-bottomed skillet over medium heat. Add the garlic, 1 teaspoon lemon zest, chile flakes and bread crumbs. The crumbs will start to fry and toast. Stir for a couple of minutes until all crumbs are toasted. Remove from heat and season to taste with salt and pepper. Drain on a brown paper bag or absorbent paper.

Rinse the Brussels sprouts. Remove the stems and cut in half. Toss the sprouts with the remaining 2 tablespoons olive oil and place on a sheet tray, cut sides down. Roast for 25 to 30 minutes—depending on the size—until browned on the sides and tender in the middle. When done place in a large bowl and toss with the pangritata, melted butter, and remaining lemon zest. Serve warm.

Cauliflower Mac and Cheese

Serves 6 to 8

3 cups panko bread crumbs

2 tablespoons melted butter, plus 3 tablespoons, divided

1 teaspoon coarse sea salt

$1/2$ teaspoon cracked black pepper

$1/4$ cup grated Parmesan cheese

$1 1/2$ pounds cauliflower florets

3 tablespoons bacon drippings

$1/4$ cup all-purpose flour

3 $1/2$ cups milk

1 tablespoon Dijon mustard

2 cups shredded Gouda cheese

2 cups shredded white cheddar cheese

$1/8$ teaspoon cayenne pepper

$1/8$ teaspoon ground nutmeg

$1/2$ cup heavy cream

1 pound elbow macaroni, cooked al dente

Preheat oven to 350 degrees F. Spray an 8 x 8-inch baking dish with nonstick spray.

In a small bowl combine the bread crumbs, 2 tablespoons melted butter, salt, pepper and Parmesan.

In a heavy-bottomed skillet add the cauliflower. Working in batches, caramelize the florets until golden brown. Set aside. In the same pot add the remaining 3 tablespoons of butter and bacon drippings; then stir in the flour to make a light roux. Cook for about 3 minutes, add the milk and mustard, and stir frequently until creamy and free of lumps, about 10 minutes. Stir in both cheeses, cayenne pepper, nutmeg, cream, and salt and pepper to taste. Cook until the cheese has melted. Stir in the pasta and cauliflower. Sprinkle with the seasoned bread crumbs and bake until bubbly and golden brown, about 25 to 30 minutes.

Crab and Artichoke Gratin

Serves 8 to 10

1/2 cup unsalted butter

1/2 cup all-purpose flour

1/4 cup minced yellow onion

1/2 cup thinly sliced green onion

3 cups heavy cream

2 tablespoons chopped parsley, plus 1 tablespoon, divided

1 cup dry white wine

1 teaspoons coarse sea salt

1/4 teaspoon white pepper

2 1/2 ounces grated Swiss cheese

6 artichokes, boiled, leaves scraped into a bowl and bottoms cut into thin slices (or substitute canned artichoke bottoms)

1 tablespoon fresh lemon juice

1/2 pound domestic mushrooms, sliced

2 pounds lump crabmeat, or 3 pounds boiled, peeled shrimp

1/4 cup grated Romano cheese

1/2 cup Panko bread crumbs

1 teaspoon paprika

Preheat oven to 350 degrees F. Spray a 3-quart casserole dish or individual ovenproof dishes with cooking spray.

To make a blond roux (see page 9), in a 2-quart saucepan over medium heat, melt the butter and stir in the flour; cook for 5 minutes. Add the minced onions and green onions. Cook for 2 to 3 minutes, until the onions are just translucent; don't let them brown. Stir in cream and parsley and cook for 3 minutes. Add the wine, salt and pepper, stir and bring to a simmer. Add the Swiss cheese and continue to stir until cheese melts. Remove pan from heat. Stir in the scrapings from the artichoke leaves, and add the artichoke bottoms, lemon juice, mushrooms, and crabmeat. Spoon into selected baking dishes and bake covered for 35 minutes. Remove from oven and sprinkle with Romano cheese and bread crumbs; bake uncovered for 5 more minutes. Garnish with paprika and remaining parsley.

Creamed Corn

Creamed corn is a great side dish, especially in the peak of summer. The key is the milking process and choosing fresh sweet corn. Try to slice off only the tips of the corn. Then use a kitchen knife to scrape the milk from the cob. I have great memories of watching my great-grandmother Dolly do this cream-style cutting. Her recipe was just pork fat, corn and a little bit of milk. She cooked it in a skillet for quite a while. She would make large batches during harvest season. I remember Uncle Walter had a big basement where all the kids would sleep downstairs during the holidays, on big feather beds alongside the places where the canned corn and summer vegetables were all shelved.

6 ears fresh white or yellow sweet corn, cleaned
   of silk

1 cup heavy cream

1 teaspoon coarse sea salt

2 tablespoons granulated sugar (optional)

$^1/_4$ teaspoon white pepper

2 tablespoons butter

1 cup milk

2 tablespoons cornstarch

$^1/_4$ cup grated Parmesan cheese

Cut the kernels from the cob and scrape the cob to extract as much of the corn milk as possible. In a saucepan over medium heat, add the whole kernels, cream, salt, sugar to taste, pepper and butter.

In a small bowl whisk together the milk and cornstarch and mix well. Stir into the corn mixture. Reduce the heat to low and cook for 10 to 15 minutes. Remove from heat and add the Parmesan; stir until melted. Check for seasonings and serve warm.

Duck Liver Dirty Rice

Serves 6 to 8

I tasted my first batch of dirty rice on a trip to Lake Charles, Louisiana, for a Zydeco music festival many years ago. We camped out overnight and woke up on Sunday morning to a wonderful smell, one so good and powerful it even conquered the smell of leftover stale beer and my rumpled campmates. There were giant pots of gumbos, cauldrons of rice dishes of all kinds, pork rinds and pots of steaming crawfish. Duck liver works best in this recipe, but if you can't find it, just substitute good-quality chicken livers to make the most of this rich and tasty fare.

1 cup duck livers

3 tablespoons bacon fat

1/2 cup minced yellow onion

1/4 cup minced red bell pepper

1/4 cup chopped green bell pepper

1/4 cup minced celery

1/2 pound Andouille sausage, casing removed

1/4 cup cubed tasso ham

2 3/4 cups chicken stock (see page 10)

1 tablespoon Kitchen Bouquet

1 dried bay leaf

Salt and ground black pepper

2 cups Uncle Ben's converted rice or brand of your choice

1/2 cup yellow corn, cooked

1/4 cup thinly sliced scallions

Preheat oven to 350 degrees F.

Clean any heavy fat and sinew from the livers. Place the bacon fat in a heavy-bottomed pan with a lid over medium-high heat. Sauté the onion, bell peppers, celery, sausage, ham and duck livers for about 10 minutes, breaking up the livers and sausage as they cook. Add the chicken stock, Kitchen Bouquet, bay leaf, and salt and pepper to taste. Bring to a boil. Stir in the rice, mixing well. Put the lid on the pot or wrap in foil and cook in the oven for 20 to 25 minutes, or until the rice is tender. Discard the bay leaf, stir in the yellow corn and scallions and serve.

Magnolias Collard Greens

Serves 6

1 tablespoon canola oil

6 ounces smoked ham hocks

1 cup diced yellow onion

1 tablespoon chopped garlic

3 tablespoon apple cider vinegar

1 tablespoon Texas Pete hot sauce

9 cups chicken stock (see page 10)

1 pound fresh collard greens, picked, washed and cut into 2-inch pieces

1 teaspoon sea salt

1 teaspoon cracked black pepper

1 small tablespoon brown sugar

Pepper vinegar for serving (optional)

Heat the oil in a large pot over medium-high heat. Add ham hocks and onion and sauté until the onion is caramelized. Add garlic and cook gently just until fragrant. Stir in the vinegar, Texas Pete and chicken stock. Bring it to a boil and add chopped collard greens; Start with about half, letting the greens wilt and cook down a bit before adding the remainder. Cook for 90 minutes, or until tender. Add more chicken stock if needed. Before removing the pot from the stove, add salt, pepper and brown sugar and give the collards a quick stir. Serve with pepper vinegar.

Potato, Leeks and Bacon

Serves 4 to 6

3 cups chicken stock

2 pounds peeled and sliced Yukon Gold potatoes

$1/2$ pound leeks, white and light green parts only, sliced lengthwise and cut into half rounds

Salt and ground black pepper

6 slices good-quality bacon, cut in $1/2$-inch pieces

2 ounces (4 tablespoons) unsalted butter

1 cup heavy cream, divided

Preheat the oven to 350 degrees F. Butter sides and bottom of a large baking dish.

In a large pot bring the chicken stock to a boil; add the potatoes and leeks. Bring back to a boil and cook for 5 minutes. Drain the potatoes into a colander, saving the stock for later.

Place one layer of drained potatoes and leeks in prepared dish, sprinkle with salt and pepper, and then add a third of the cream, another layer of potatoes and leeks, salt and pepper and half of remaining cream. Top with bacon and salt and pepper to taste. Pour in $1 1/2$ cups stock and top with rest of the cream. Wrap with foil and bake for 35 minutes covered and 15 minutes uncovered.

Crookneck Squash and Onions

Serves 4 to 6

1 tablespoon bacon drippings

1 cup thin half-round slices Vidalia onion

2 pounds yellow squash, halved and sliced into 1-inch pieces

Pinch of sugar

3 cup chicken stock (see page 10)

2 tablespoons butter

Salt and ground black pepper

In a medium-sized skillet melt the bacon drippings. Add the onion and sauté until translucent, about 5 minutes. Add the squash, sugar and chicken stock and cook covered over low heat for 35 minutes, stirring several times. Add butter and salt and pepper to taste. Serve warm.

Rosemary-Parmesan Potatoes

Serves 6

3 large Russet potatoes, peeled and diced into 1-inch cubes

3 tablespoons olive oil

2 tablespoons chopped fresh rosemary

1 cup grated Parmesan cheese

1 tablespoon chopped garlic

Sea salt and ground black pepper

Preheat oven to 400 degrees F.

Boil a pot of water large enough to hold the potatoes. Once the water has come to a boil, add potatoes and cook for about 5 minutes. Pour the potatoes into a colander and drain well.

In a cast iron skillet or large ovenproof pan, heat the olive oil. Add potatoes and roast in the oven or on top of the stove until just fork-tender. A minute or two before the potatoes are done, add rosemary, cheese and garlic. Season with salt and pepper to taste. Serve hot.

South Carolina White Rice

Makes 4 cups

1 tablespoon olive oil or butter

1 small yellow onion, minced

1 1/2 cups Carolina or jasmine rice

3 cups chicken stock (see page 10) or water

1 dried bay leaf

1-2 pinches of coarse sea salt

1 tablespoon salted butter

Heat the olive oil or butter in a medium saucepan and sauté the onion until translucent, about 5 minutes. Add the rice to the pan and stir; sauté for about 2 minutes, until the rice is coated. Add the chicken stock and bring to a boil, then add the bay leaf and salt. Cover the pan with a lid. Reduce the heat to low and cook for 15 to 18 minutes, until rice is tender to the bite. Remove pan from heat, add the salted butter and fluff the rice with a fork. Serve immediately or spread on a sheet tray to cool, then store for later use.

Southern-Style Pole Beans

Serves 6

This recipe comes from Jeremy Ashby.

2 yellow or sweet onions, quartered

Bundle of fresh thyme

Bundle of fresh sage

1 smoked ham hock, country ham scraps or
    smoked bacon (about 6–8 ounces)

1 tablespoon sea salt

4 cloves garlic, halved

2 quarts water

2 pounds pole beans, strings removed

Combine the onions, herbs, pork, salt and garlic in a medium pot. Add water and bring to a boil. Turn heat down to a simmer and cook uncovered for 45 minutes. Add the beans and cook uncovered until tender, about 25 minutes. Scoop the beans from the broth and transfer to a large serving bowl. Continue to cook the broth until reduced by half, and then pour the hot broth over the beans in the serving bowl.

Spicy Black Beans

Makes 5 cups

I always keep a few quarts of cooked beans in the freezer to serve over rice, or with chicken and tacos. They freeze well in heavy-duty ziplock bags or freezer containers.

1 pound black turtle beans

1 tablespoon olive oil

2 cups diced yellow onion

2 smoked ham hocks

2 cloves garlic, minced

2 tablespoons minced jalapeño

10 cups water

1 teaspoon freshly ground black pepper, plus
    more for seasoning

Pinch of cayenne pepper

Coarse sea salt

Pour the beans onto a rimmed sheet tray and remove any rocks, pebbles or foreign matter. Rinse beans in a colander with cold water and set aside.

In a large stockpot over medium heat, add the olive oil and sauté the onion, ham hocks, garlic and jalapeño until onion is translucent. Add the beans, water, 1 teaspoon black pepper and cayenne. Bring to a boil, then reduce heat to a simmer and cook uncovered for 2 1/2 to 3 hours, until the beans are soft. More water may be needed if the beans have cooked quickly. When the beans are cooked and softened, taste and adjust salt and pepper as needed.

Summer Beans and Peas

Serves 6

Butter beans, zipper peas, baby lima beans, speckled butter beans, cranberry beans, cow peas and black-eyed peas are just a few of the local varieties around Charleston. Fresh from the fields, they're part of the delicious Lowcountry cuisine that we love. They all take around 30 to 35 minutes to cook. You might need to add a little more water for this step too.

4 cups fresh beans or peas

4 thick-cut pieces of bacon or a smoked ham hock (about 6–8 ounces)

1 tablespoon olive oil

1/2 cup diced yellow onion

4 cups water

3 tablespoons butter

3/4 teaspoon salt

Dash of white pepper

Rinse the beans and peas in a colander under cold water, carefully inspecting the beans to remove foreign particles. Place a medium-sized pot on medium heat, add the bacon or smoked pork product, olive oil and onion. Sauté for 3 to 5 minutes. Add water and bring it up to a boil. Turn heat down to a simmer and cook for about 45 minutes. Add peas or beans and cook for about 30 minutes, or until tender. As the beans cook, a foam will appear on top. Use a spoon to scrape off the foam and discard it. When done, scoop the peas or beans from the broth and transfer to a large serving bowl and keep warm. Continue to cook the broth until reduced by half. Add butter, salt and pepper. (For a little more creaminess, add about a cup of the beans or peas back to the broth and mash a few of the beans or peas to give the mix a little more body.) Pour the hot broth over the peas or beans in the serving bowl. For a true southern treat, enjoy the beans or peas with a piping-hot slice of cornbread and butter.

Twice-Baked New Potatoes

Family Style

---

3 pounds new potatoes, about 30

4 ounces chopped bacon or pancetta

1/3 cup heavy cream

2 teaspoons truffle oil, plus 1 tablespoon, divided

1/3 cup sour cream

2 tablespoons chopped sage leaves

1 teaspoon coarse sea salt

1/4 teaspoon ground black pepper

1/2 cup grated Parmesan cheese

1 tablespoon chopped chives

1 black truffle (optional), thinly sliced

Heat the oven to 350 degrees F.

Place the potatoes on a baking tray and bake until soft when pierced with a fork, about 25 to 30 minutes.

Place a small skillet over medium heat and sauté the bacon until crisp, about 4 to 5 minutes. When potatoes are cool enough to handle, cut the very bottoms off so they will stand straight on a plate, then halve. Using a melon baller, scoop out of the centers, reserving about a 1/8-inch border to keep the potatoes stable. Place the potato pulp into a ricer or food mill with a fine disk. Heat the

heavy cream, 2 teaspoons truffle oil, sour cream, and sage in a small saucepot until warm. Fold into the riced potatoes. Add bacon and season with salt and pepper.

Using a pastry bag or spoon, fill about 2 dozen of the scooped-out potatoes, using only the best-looking ones; discard the rest. Garnish with Parmesan cheese. Bake at 350 degrees F for 10 to 15 minutes, or until warm and slightly browned. Drizzle with remaining tablespoon of truffle oil and sprinkle with chopped chives and shaved truffles, if desired.

Sweet Potato and Cherry Hash

Serves 6

This recipe is from Magnolias alumni Scott Popovic. Scott was previously the executive chef for Certified Angus Beef but is currently the head chef/partner at Bacchanalia in Cleveland, Ohio. This side dish is a great accompaniment to roasted poultry or duck.

3/4 pound bacon, sliced and chopped into 1/4-inch uniform cubes

3 large sweet potatoes (2 pounds), peeled and diced medium

2 shallots, sliced

12 ounces frozen cherries, cooked down to reduce moisture

2 tablespoons chopped parsley

Salt and ground black pepper

Render the bacon in a large sauté pan until partially cooked; remove from pan. Add the sweet potatoes to bacon drippings and cook over medium-high heat until soft. Add shallots, bacon and cherries to potato mixture and continue to cook until shallots are translucent. Toss in the chopped parsley and salt and pepper to taste. Serve warm.

DESSERTS

Chocolate Crème Brûlée with Orange-Cinnamon Snaps

Serves 6

1 quart heavy cream

1 teaspoon pure vanilla extract

2 tablespoons cocoa powder

$1/2$ cup granulated sugar, divided

12 egg yolks

8 ounces semisweet chocolate chips

BRÛLÉE TOPPING

$1/2$ cup packed light brown sugar

$1/2$ cup granulated sugar

Orange cinnamon snaps (recipe follows)

Preheat the oven to 285 degrees F. Prepare an ice bath.

Combine the cream, vanilla, cocoa powder and half of the sugar in a saucepan; bring to boil and remove from heat.

Meanwhile, in a separate large bowl whisk together the egg yolks and remaining $1/4$ cup sugar until well combined.

Heat the cream mixture over medium heat until there are small bubbles around the edges of the pan. Slowly stream hot cream into the egg yolk mixture, stirring constantly. When half the cream is incorporated, slowly pour mixture back into the pan of hot cream, stirring constantly. Add the chocolate chips and stir until melted, then strain into a container, skimming off any foam. Set the mixture in an ice bath to chill.

Pour the mixture into 6 brûlée dishes or ramekins and place in a roasting pan with deep sides. Place the pan on the middle rack of the oven. Pull the rack out and add enough hot water to come halfway up the sides of the dishes. Carefully slide the rack back in and cook for 40 to 45 minutes, rotating the pan halfway through cooking. The custards are set when a knife point inserted into the center comes out clean. Carefully pull the rack from the oven and lift ramekins from the water using a spatula and towel. Place on a rack to cool for a couple of hours or overnight.

Pour off any moisture that might have accumulated on top of the brûlées. Mix the two sugars together. Sprinkle a light layer of sugar on the brûlées. Using a hand-held self-igniting torch, flame the tops directly to caramelize the sugar and lightly burn the cream. Serve immediately and garnish with an orange-cinnamon snap.

Orange-Cinnamon Snaps

Makes 2 dozen

4 cups all-purpose flour

2 teaspoons baking powder

2 teaspoons ground cinnamon

1 teaspoon fine sea salt

12 ounces unsalted butter

$^1/_2$ cup honey

2 cups granulated sugar

2 whole eggs

Zest of 1 orange

Preheat oven to 350 degrees F. Sift together the dry ingredients. Beat together the butter, honey and sugar until light and creamy. Scrape down the bowl and add the eggs. Add the sifted dry ingredients and the orange zest and mix until well incorporated. Scoop onto a greased cookie sheet and bake until golden brown, about 10 to 12 minutes. Let cool on a rack.

Apple and Oatmeal Crunch with Cinnamon Ice Cream

Serves 6

7 large apples

4 ounces unsalted butter, plus 4 ounces chilled and cubed

4 ounces light brown sugar

1 tablespoon ground cinnamon

1 teaspoon ground nutmeg, divided

$1/4$ teaspoon ground cardamom

$1/2$ cup all-purpose flour

1 cup rolled oats

$1/4$ cup granulated sugar

Cinnamon ice cream (recipe follows)

Preheat oven to 350 degrees F. Spray an 8-inch ovenproof baking dish with nonstick spray.

Peel, core and cut apples into 1-inch cubes. Melt 4 ounces of butter and brown sugar in a large sauté pan. Add the apples, cinnamon, and half the nutmeg and toss the apples with a spoon until well coated. Cook for 2 minutes then remove from heat and cool. Cut the remaining chilled butter into small dice. Place in a mixer or food processor and add the cardamom, remaining nutmeg, flour, oats and sugar. Mix on low speed until mixture is crumbly. Place the apples in prepared baking dish and top with oat mixture. Bake until bubbly and brown, about 35 to 40 minutes. Serve warm with cinnamon ice cream.

Cinnamon Ice Cream

Makes 1 quart

3 cups half & half

2 cups cinnamon, vanilla sugar (see page 19) or plain granulated sugar, divided

$1 1/2$ teaspoon ground cinnamon

3 whole cinnamon sticks

1 whole vanilla bean split in half

10 egg yolks

3 cups heavy cream

In a large saucepan over medium heat, combine the half & half and 1 cup of sugar. Mix well and add the cinnamon, cinnamon sticks and vanilla bean. Stir and bring to a high simmer, but do not boil.

In a separate bowl add the egg yolks and remaining 1 cup of sugar and beat well.

Remove and discard cinnamon sticks and vanilla bean pod, but scrape the bean for any remaining seeds and add back to the cream mixture. The next step is to temper the egg yolks: dip a ladle of the half & half mixture and add to the yolks, beating well. Add one more ladle and mix well again. Reduce heat to medium low and add the egg mixture back into the half & half; whisk until smooth and thick enough to coat the back of a spoon. Add the heavy cream. Stir well and then chill for 1 hour. Process in an ice cream machine according to the manufacturer's directions. Chill overnight.

Chocolate Drop Oatmeal Cookies *Makes 4 dozen*

1/2 cup shortening

1/2 cup packed brown sugar

1/2 cup granulated sugar

1 egg

1 teaspoon vanilla extract

3/4 cup all-purpose flour

1/2 teaspoon baking soda

1/2 teaspoon fine sea salt

1 1/2 cups rolled oats

1/2 cup chopped raisins, chopped

1/2 cup semisweet chocolate chips

Preheat oven to 350 degrees F. Grease a baking sheet.

Cream together shortening and sugars. Add the egg and vanilla and beat well. Sift together flour, soda and salt onto a piece of wax paper. Add the sifted dry ingredients to the creamed shortening, then add the oats, raisins and chocolate chips. Mix well. Drop by the rounded tablespoon onto baking sheet or use a #30 scoop. Bake for 10 minutes, until lightly golden.

Pecan Pie *Makes 1 pie*

PIE DOUGH

3/4 cups all-purpose flour

1/4 teaspoon baking powder

Pinch of salt

4 tablespoons cold butter, cut into small chunks

3 tablespoons cold water

FILLING

3 eggs

1/2 cup dark brown corn syrup

1/2 cups light corn syrup

1/4 cup sugar

1/2 cup (1 stick) butter, melted

Pinch of salt

1 teaspoon vanilla extract

2 cups pecans, lightly toasted

PIE DOUGH: Mix the flour, baking powder, salt and butter until the butter forms pea-sized pieces. Add the cold water all at once and stir just until the dough comes together. Wrap in plastic wrap and refrigerate for about 3 hours or overnight. Roll out the dough and fit into pie pan. Place in the freezer for 15 minutes or until time to bake the pie.

FILLING: Preheat the oven to 350 degrees F. In a medium-sized bowl, whisk together all the ingredients except pecans. Place pecans in the bottom of a 9-inch unbaked pie shell. Pour the filling into the shell and bake for approximately 50 minutes, until the custard has set, rotating the pie halfway through cooking.

Coconut Cake

It's a sweet southern favorite. The cake has several steps but is quite simple to prepare. Both the cake and pastry cream can be made a day or two ahead, but prepare the frosting as a final step when you're ready to assemble the cake.

3 cups cake flour, sifted

2 $^1/_4$ teaspoons baking powder

$^1/_2$ teaspoon baking soda

$^1/_4$ teaspoon fine sea salt

2 sticks unsalted butter (Plugra brand), room temperature

16 ounces or 1 box powdered sugar, sifted

4 large egg yolks, room temperature

2 teaspoons vanilla extract

1 teaspoon coconut extract

$^1/_2$ cup sour cream

$^3/_4$ cup milk, room temperature

1 $^1/_3$ cups sweetened flaked coconut

4 large egg whites, room temperature

2 tablespoons granulated sugar

$^1/_8$ teaspoon cream of tartar

TO FINISH

Pastry cream (recipe follows)

Coconut frosting (recipe follows)

3 cups lightly toasted unsweetened shredded coconut

Lightly butter and flour three 9-inch cake pans. Line the bottom with parchment or circles of waxed paper and set aside. Preheat the oven to 350 degrees F.

Sift the flour, baking powder, soda and salt onto a large sheet of waxed paper and set aside. In the bowl of a stand mixer fitted with a paddle attachment, cream the butter on moderately high speed for 3 minutes. Reduce the speed to moderate and beat in the powdered sugar in 4 additions, blending well and scraping down the sides of the mixing bowl frequently. Continue beating for 3 more minutes on moderately high speed, until light and fluffy. Beat in the egg yolks one at a time, blending well after each addition. Blend in the vanilla and coconut extracts. Turn the speed to low and add the sifted flour mixture in 3 additions, alternating with the sour cream and milk in 2 additions, ending with the flour mixture. Fold in the coconut by hand.

In a clean mixing bowl, whip the egg whites with the granulated sugar until frothy; add the cream

of tartar and continue beating until moist, firm peaks are formed. Gently fold half of the beaten egg whites into the cake mixture to lighten it, then add the remaining egg whites. Divide the batter among the 3 pans.

Place two baking racks so they divide the oven into thirds. Bake cakes for 30 to 35 minutes. To ensure even baking, turn the pans and rotate them on the oven racks about three-quarters of the way through the cooking time. Test for doneness with a toothpick inserted in the center; it should come out clean and dry. Remove the pans from the oven and let cool completely. Run a thin flexible knife along the sides of the pans and invert onto a rack. Peel off the waxed paper. Place cakes in the freezer for a few minutes to better prepare for slicing. Using a long serrated knife, slice each cake into 2 even layers to produce a total of 6 layers.

Place one cake layer on a cake stand or plate and spread a $1/2$-inch layer of the pastry cream over the cake. Repeat with the remaining layers, leaving the top layer plain. Refrigerate the cake while you make the frosting. Remove cake from refrigerator and, working quickly, frost the top and sides of the cake. Sprinkle the toasted coconut heavily over the top and sides to finish.

Pastry Cream

Enough for 1 cake

1 $1/2$ cups sweetened shredded coconut, sweetened

4 cups half & half

$1/2$ cup cornstarch

1 $1/8$ cup granulated sugar

7 large egg yolks

1 teaspoon vanilla extract

5 tablespoons cold unsalted butter (Plugra brand), diced

To make the pastry cream, process shredded coconut in the food processor until finely chopped. In a large saucepot combine the half & half with coconut and bring to a low simmer. Remove from heat and let the coconut infuse into the cream for 20 minutes. In a small bowl combine the cornstarch and sugar, whisking until lump free, and set aside.

Next, temper the eggs yolks. In a medium-sized bowl beat the egg yolks. Bring the half & half mixture back to a high simmer. Whisk the cornstarch into the egg yolks a little at a time until the mixture is thick and smooth. Slowly add 1 cup of the hot half & half into the egg mixture, whisking constantly to temper the eggs. Whisk the tempered eggs back into the remaining half & half. Cook over medium-high heat for 10 minutes (do not let it boil). Remove from heat and whisk in the vanilla and butter. Transfer to a medium-sized bowl, cover with plastic wrap and allow to chill overnight or at least 4 to 5 hours.

Coconut Frosting

Enough for 1 cake

4 large egg whites

$3/4$ cup granulated or vanilla-scented sugar (see page 19)

1 teaspoon vanilla extract

$1/8$ teaspoon fine sea salt

$1/3$ cup light corn syrup plus 2 tablespoons

Combine the egg whites, sugar, vanilla and salt in a large heatproof bowl. Using a double-boiler method, set the bowl in a saucepan over barely simmering water and beat with a hand mixer on medium speed for 6 minutes. Add the corn syrup and turn the mixer to medium high and continue beating for 1 to 2 minutes, until the frosting has doubled in size and is shiny. Remove from the water bath and beat 1 minute more to cool the frosting.

Flourless Chocolate-Espresso Torte

Serves 8

This recipe is from Mike Dolberg, a Magnolias alumnus and friend, who is a big Carolina Gamecocks fan. When he was single, this was his go-to dessert, but now he's off the market. It worked for him—it might work for you too!

¹/₂ cup water	1 cup unsalted butter
2 tablespoons fresh-ground espresso	3 eggs
³/₄ cup sugar	3 egg whites
Pinch of salt	Raspberry sauce (recipe follows)
14 ounces bittersweet chocolate	Powdered sugar for garnishing

Preheat oven to 325 degrees F. Lightly butter a 9-inch springform pan and place a circle of buttered parchment paper inside.

In a small saucepan over medium-low heat, add the water, espresso, sugar and salt; stir until dissolved. Set aside.

Melt the chocolate in the microwave for about 15 seconds, stir, and then microwave for 15 seconds more, or until melted. In the bowl of a stand mixer with a paddle attachment, add the melted chocolate and slowly add the butter, a little at a time; mix on low speed until well incorporated. Slowly beat in the sugar mixture then add the eggs and egg whites one at a time, scraping down the bowl as you go.

Fold the mixture into the prepared springform pan and smooth the top with a spatula. Wrap well with foil to prevent water leaks in the next step. Take a pan larger than your 9-inch springform pan and fill it halfway with hot water. Place the springform pan in the hot water bath.

Bake in the preheated oven for about 40 minutes. The center will still be a little soft. Remove from the oven and water bath. Leave the cake in the pan and refrigerate for at least 6 hours or overnight. When cool, place the bottom of the pan in warm water for 10 seconds to help release the cake. Run a warm knife around the sides. Remove the foil and release the latch on the pan. Invert the cake onto a plate and remove the parchment paper. Mike serves this with raspberry sauce and powdered sugar.

Raspberry Sauce

Makes 2 cups

¹/₄ cup sugar	1 teaspoon fresh lemon juice
¹/₂ pint fresh raspberries	1 cup raspberry jam

Combine sugar, fresh raspberries and lemon juice in a small saucepan over medium heat and simmer until the sugar is dissolved. Add the raspberry jam and cook for 5 minutes. Remove from heat. If you don't mind seeds you can chill and store in an airtight container until ready to serve. Otherwise, place all the above ingredients in a food processor fitted with a metal blade and blend until smooth. Strain to remove seeds before storing. Bring to room temperature before serving.

Plantation Rice Tarts *Makes 6 (4 1/2-inch) tarts or 1 (8-inch) tart shell*

TART SHELLS

1/2 cup vanilla sugar (see page 19) or granulated sugar

1/4 teaspoon fine sea salt

1/2 cup softened butter

1 teaspoon vanilla extract

1/2 teaspoon almond extract

1 1/2 cups unbleached all-purpose flour

3/4 cup almond flour

TART FILLING

3 1/2 cups milk

1 1/4 cups water

1/2 cup plus 2 tablespoons lemon sugar (see page 19)

2 strips lemon peel

Pinch of fine sea salt

1 1/8 cups long-grain rice

1 rounded cup raisins

1/3 cup rum plus 2 tablespoons, divided

2 large eggs, separated

1 1/4 teaspoons vanilla extract

5 tablespoons unsalted butter (Plugra brand)

TART SHELLS: Preheat oven to 350 degrees F. Spray tart pans with nonstick spray.

To make the crust using a stand mixer, on medium speed beat together the sugar, salt, butter and extracts. Turn the speed to low and add both flours; mix just until the batter comes together. Press the crumbs into tart pans. Prick the tarts all over with a fork and place in the freezer for 15 minutes. Then bake the tarts just until they begin to brown on the edges, about 10 minutes. Remove from oven and let cool while you prepare the filling.

TART FILLING: Heat the milk, water, lemon sugar, lemon peel and salt in a medium-sized saucepan over medium heat; bring to a boil. Stir in the rice and reduce the heat to low. Cook covered, stirring occasionally, until all the liquid has been absorbed, about 20 to 25 minutes. Spread the rice on a sheet pan, remove the lemon peel and cool rice to room temperature.

Soak the raisins in 1/3 cup of rum for at least 30 minutes. In a medium-sized bowl whisk the egg yolks and vanilla together. Stir in the rice, butter and raisins with rum and mix thoroughly. Beat the egg whites until stiff but moist peaks form. Fold into the rice mixture. Pour the mixture into the tart shells. Bake for 20 minutes. If the tops are too pale, brown beneath the broiler. Brush the tops with the remaining rum. Serve at room temperature.

Ice cream just has to be one of the best desserts of all time. You can buy great commercially prepared ice cream from just about any grocery store, but nothing beats good homemade ice cream. There are so many kinds, too, from French vanilla to Italian sorbets. You can use milk and eggs or half milk, half cream, and eggs. Various recipes call for evaporated milk, full heavy cream, buttermilk, or powdered milk. But each ingredient has its own use.

We use three different kinds of ice cream. One is custard-based, the second mousse-based and the third sorbet-based.

It's important that you follow the manufacturer's procedures when churning the ice cream and let the flavors ripen for a couple of hours before you enjoy a frosty bowlful. Most homemade ice cream freezes harder than commercial brands, so bring it out to thaw a little before serving.

Standard Vanilla Custard Ice Cream

Makes 1 quart custard base

1 1/2 cups heavy cream

1 cup whole milk

1/2 vanilla bean or 1 teaspoon vanilla extract

2 whole eggs

2 egg yolks

3/4 cup sugar

1/4 teaspoon fine sea salt

If recommended in the ice cream maker's use and handling instructions, place your ice cream machine canister in the freezer.

In a heavy-bottomed saucepot over medium-low heat, bring the cream, milk and vanilla bean to a high simmer for 5 minutes. Remove from heat and remove the vanilla bean, scrape the seeds and return them to the cream.

Beat the eggs, egg yolks, sugar and salt together in a heatproof bowl until thick and mousse-like. Next, temper the eggs with the hot milk by slowly streaming the milk into the egg mixture, whisking the whole time. Place the bowl over a hot-water bath and cook until thick and creamy. Quickly remove from heat and chill in an ice-water bath, stirring occasionally. Pour the mixture into your machine canister and process according to manufacturer's directions.

Standard French Vanilla Mousse Ice Cream

Makes 3 cups

1 ³/₄ cups heavy cream
¹/₂ vanilla bean or 1 teaspoon vanilla extract
¹/₂ cup water

¹/₄ cup sugar
3 egg yolks

If required by the manufacturer, place your canister in the freezer.

In a heavy-bottomed saucepot over medium heat, bring the cream and vanilla bean to a high simmer for 5 minutes. DO NOT BOIL. Remove from heat.

Place the water and sugar in another heavy-bottomed saucepot over medium-high heat and bring to a boil, dissolving the sugar and boiling for 5 minutes. Allow to cool for 45 seconds.

Beat the egg yolks until yellowish, pale and frothy. Pour the hot sugar syrup slowly over the egg, whisking constantly until thickened.

Strain the cream and remove the vanilla bean; scrape the seeds into the cream. Add to the egg mixture and whisk until frothy, about 3 minutes. Pour into the ice cream canister and follow the manufacturer's instructions. Once churned, transfer ice cream to a freezer-safe container and freeze overnight or until firm enough to scoop.

{ FLAVORED ICE CREAMS }

Use peaches, strawberries, blackberries or any fruit combination.

Make up a batch of mousse or custard ice cream and freeze according to specifications. When frozen, stir in 1 ¹/₂ cups mashed ripe fruit. Place back into the machine and process on normal settings. Once churned, transfer the ice cream to a freezer-safe container and freeze overnight or until firm enough to scoop.

NUT-FLAVORED OR LIQUEUR-FLAVORED ICE CREAM

Use any variety of nuts and flavoring, such as coffee or espresso, almonds, pecans, walnuts, coconut, bourbon, Baileys Irish Cream, Kahlúa, Earl Gray tea or green tea.

Use either ice cream recipe (custard or mousse), but add the ground nuts, coffee, liqueur, or green tea ingredients to the cream first and let it steep or dissolve. Then strain the hot cream before adding to the egg mixture.

If you want to add additions such as chocolate, cookies, candy bars or candied nuts, just chop and add them during the last few minutes of churning. When finished, transfer to freezer-safe container and freeze overnight or until firm enough to scoop.

Key Lime Pie

Makes 1 (9-inch) pie

PIE CRUST

1 1/2 cups graham cracker crumbs

2 1/2 tablespoons granulated sugar

1/2 cup ground pecans

1/8 cup shredded sweetened coconut

1/2 cup sweet butter, melted

KEY LIME CURD FILLING

1/2 cup sweet butter, melted

Juice of 6 Key limes

1 teaspoon grated lime zest

1 1/4 cup powdered sugar

4 large beaten eggs

PIE CRUST: Preheat the oven to 325 degrees F. Mix together the graham cracker crumbs, sugar, pecans and coconut. Add the melted butter, mixing well. Put the mixture into a 9-inch pie pans and mold against the sides and bottom. Bake for 5 minutes. Cool to room temperature and then refrigerate.

KEY LIME CURD FILLING: To prepare the filling, heat the butter, Key lime juice, zest and sugar in a double boiler over low heat; cook until sugar is dissolved and gently stir continuously. Whisk in the beaten eggs and continue to cook, stirring continuously, for about 5 minutes more, or until thickened. Remove from heat and transfer to a metal bowl, then place in an ice-water bath to chill. Once chilled, spoon the mixture into pie shell and refrigerate for 2 hours.

Whipped Cream Topping

Serves 8

1 cup heavy cream

2 tablespoons powdered sugar

1 teaspoon vanilla extract

Using a stand mixer with a wire whisk, combine all ingredients and whip on medium-high speed to firm peaks.

Red Velvet Cake

Over the years we've made many different varieties of red velvet cakes, from Twinkies and red velvet whoopie pies to bread pudding and cookies. Originally, I think, shredded beets and cocoa powder were used to produce the deep ruby-chocolate color, but we use red food coloring. Traditional and time-honored frostings can vary just as much as the cake recipes, with some using a buttercream or cream cheese, while some call for an old-fashioned boiled milk recipe with flour, butter, sugar and vanilla extract. Here we combine the best of all worlds.

2 $^1/_2$ cups sifted cake flour

2 tablespoons cocoa powder

$^1/_2$ teaspoon fine sea salt

$^1/_2$ cup unsalted butter

1 $^1/_2$ cups vanilla sugar (see page 19) or granulated sugar

1 teaspoon real vanilla extract

2 large eggs

2 tablespoons red liquid food coloring

1 cup buttermilk

1 teaspoon baking soda

1 teaspoon red wine vinegar

Frosting (recipe follows)

Preheat oven to 350 degrees F and butter two 9-inch cake pans and line with circles of parchment paper.

Over a medium-sized bowl, sift together the cake flour, cocoa powder and salt; set aside. In a stand mixer fitted with a metal blade, cream the butter. Add the sugar and vanilla and beat for 3 minutes. Add the eggs one at a time, scraping down the bowl after each addition.

In a measuring cup add the 2 tablespoons of red food coloring and buttermilk and mix well to combine, exercising caution to prevent spillage. Turn mixer to low speed and add one-third of the flour mixture. Then add half of the buttermilk, another third of the flour mixture, the rest of the buttermilk and the remainder of the flour mixture, in that order.

Place the soda in a small cup or bowl and add the red wine vinegar. Mix it quickly and add to the cake batter. Quickly pour the batter into the prepared cake pans, dividing equally between pans. Place on the center rack of the oven and bake for 25 to 30 minutes, or until a toothpick inserted in the middle of the cake comes out clean. Cool the pans for 10 minutes and then invert onto a cake rack or plate to cool. When cooled, wrap in plastic and refrigerate for at least 4 hours or overnight.

TO ASSEMBLE: Halve each cake layer with a serrated knife to make four layers. Place one layer on a cake stand or plate and spread about $1/4$ inch of icing on top. Repeat with the remaining layers. Ice the top and sprinkle with candied chopped pecans.

Vanilla Bean Frosting

Enough for 1 cake

2 vanilla beans split in half

4 cups whole milk

12 tablespoons all-purpose flour

2 pounds (8 sticks) unsalted butter (Plugra brand)

4 cups sugar

2 teaspoon pure vanilla extract

2 teaspoons almond extract

2 cups chopped candied pecans for garnish (see page 77)

In a medium-sized saucepan over medium-low heat, steep the vanilla beans in warm milk for 5 minutes. Scrape the inside of the beans into the milk and discard the pods. Before adding the flour, it's best to make a slurry using $1/4$ cup of the warm milk and all the flour, to prevent clumping. Gradually whisk in the flour mixture over medium heat, whisking constantly until thickened and smooth. Cook for 12 to 15 minutes to remove the raw flour taste. Strain to remove any lumps, place in a bowl and cover with plastic wrap directly on the surface to prevent a film from forming. Set aside and let cool to room temperature for about 45 minutes. In the bowl of a stand mixer fitted with a paddle attachment, beat the butter on medium-high for 4 minutes, until smooth and creamy. Slowly add the sugar and beat for 4 minutes. Add the vanilla and almond extracts and beat 1 minute more. Add the cooled milk-and-flour mixture slowly into the bowl, mixing on moderately high speed for 5 minutes. The frosting will get progressively whiter. Cover and refrigerate immediately. Let sit for 15 minutes, then use right away.

Red Velvet Bread Pudding

Serves 8

RED VELVET CAKE

8 ounces (2 sticks) butter, room temperature

3 cups granulated sugar

4 eggs

8 tablespoons liquid red food coloring

2 1/2 teaspoons vanilla extract

3 1/2 cups all-purpose flour

4 tablespoons cocoa powder, sifted

2 teaspoons salt

2 cups buttermilk

2 1/2 teaspoons baking soda

2 1/2 teaspoons cider vinegar

RED VELVET BREAD PUDDING MIX

6 ounces cream cheese, room temperature

3/4 cup sugar

1 1/4 cup milk

1 1/4 cup heavy cream

Pinch of salt

2 eggs

2 egg yolks

1 teaspoon vanilla extract

RED VELVET CAKE: Preheat oven to 325 degrees F. Spray and flour two 9-inch cake pans or an 11 x 17-inch sheet pan. Using a stand mixer with paddle attachment, beat together the butter and sugar until light and fluffy, about 5 minutes. Add the eggs one at a time, scraping the bowl throughout this process to make sure there are no lumps.

In a separate small bowl mix together the food coloring and vanilla, then add it to the butter mixture.

Sift together the flour, cocoa powder and salt. Starting with the flour mixture, add the flour and then buttermilk to the butter mixture, alternating in three additions each. Continue to scrape the bowl to avoid lumps. Combine the baking soda and the vinegar and stir into the batter thoroughly. Pour the batter into prepared pan(s).

Bake 9-inch pans for approximately 30 minutes or the sheet pan for about 20 minutes, until the cake springs back when tapped lightly and a cake tester inserted in the center comes out clean.

RED VELVET BREAD PUDDING MIX: Preheat oven to 325 degrees. Prepare 8 (6-ounce) ramekins with nonstick spray.

Using a stand mixer with paddle attachment, beat the cream cheese and sugar together until smooth.

In a separate mixing bowl whisk the milk, cream, salt, eggs, egg yolks, and vanilla until completely combined. Add a small amount of the milk mixture to the cream cheese while the mixer is running. Scrape it down and mix until smooth. Then gradually add the rest of the milk mixture to the cream cheese, a little at a time. Keep scraping the sides of the bowl to avoid lumps and to achieve a smooth custard filling.

TO ASSEMBLE: Cut the cake into small chunks and fill each ramekin or desired container. Pour bread pudding mix over cake to fill containers about three-quarters full. Let the cake stand for about 30 minutes to absorb some of the liquid. Top off the bread puddings with a little bit more mix, and then bake in a water bath in a 325-degree oven. Cooking times will vary from 30 to 50 minutes depending on the size of your containers.

Peach Buttermilk Sherbet

Serves 4 to 6

1 cup puréed fresh or frozen peaches

$1/3$ cup sugar, more or less

2 tablespoons lemon juice

Pinch of fine sea salt

$1 1/2$ cups buttermilk

Using a blender or food processor, combine the peaches, $1/3$ cup sugar, lemon juice, salt, and buttermilk, stirring well until the sugar dissolves. Add more or less sugar depending on your taste. The flavor should be sharp but not sweet. Transfer to the ice cream machine and process according to manufacturer's directions. When finished, use a spatula to transfer sherbet into a freezer-safe container and freeze overnight or until firm enough to scoop.

Watermelon Ice

Serves 4 to 6

4 cups seedless watermelon

$1/2$ cup sugar

Juice of 1 lemon

Place watermelon in a blender for 35 seconds and blend on high speed. Combine sugar and lemon juice, add to the watermelon purée and blend for 30 seconds. Pass through a strainer and place into an ice cream freezer. Freeze according to manufacturer's recommendations. Remove and store in a freezer-proof container overnight or until firm enough to scoop.

Strawberry Sherbet

Serves 4 to 6

2 pounds cleaned strawberries

Juice of 1 lemon

Juice of 1 orange

1 3/4 cups sugar

1/2 cup water

Blend or purée the fruit and push through a strainer; add the lemon and orange juice.

Combine the sugar and water in a small heavy-bottomed saucepot and bring to a slow boil; cook for 3 minutes. Combine the fruit purée and sugar syrup and place in the ice cream freezer. Freeze according to manufacturer's directions. Remove and store in a freezer-proof container and freeze overnight or until firm enough to scoop.

Orange Sorbet

Serves 4 to 6

1 1/2 cups orange juice, strained

Grated rind of 1 small orange (no white pith)

3/4 cup carbonated mineral water

1 cup sugar

Juice from 2 lemons, strained

1 egg white

Mix the orange juice with the grated rind and set aside.

Place water and sugar into a heavy-bottomed saucepan and slowly bring to a boil, cooking for 5 minutes. Remove from heat and cool. Add the lemon juice to the orange juice and blend well.

Beat the egg white with 2 tablespoons of the orange juice mixture until frothy, and then fold back into the orange juice mixture and place in an ice cream freezer. Freeze according to manufacturer's directions. Remove and freeze in a freezer-proof container overnight or until firm enough to scoop.

Warm Peach Pound Cake

Makes 1 cake

When Carolina peaches come into season, the bakers among us will whip up half a dozen pound cakes at a time. For individual desserts you can use single-serving ramekins or custard dishes. Cook the single servings at the same temperature but for only 10 to 12 minutes. I like to serve this with vanilla bean ice cream and warm caramelized peaches.

PEACH POUND CAKE

1 cup (2 sticks) unsalted butter

2 cups granulated sugar

4 large eggs

1/4 teaspoon almond extract

1 teaspoon vanilla extract

2 3/4 cups, plus 1/4 cup all-purpose flour, divided

1 teaspoon baking powder

1/4 teaspoon ground cinnamon

1/4 teaspoon ground nutmeg

1/4 teaspoon ground ginger

1/2 teaspoon fine sea salt

2 cups chopped fresh peaches

1/4 cup powdered sugar

Preheat the oven to 325 degrees F. Butter a loaf pan or a Bundt cake pan and coat with sugar. In large mixing bowl, cream butter and sugar until light and fluffy. Add the eggs one at a time, beating well after each addition; then add the almond and vanilla extracts.

In a separate bowl sift together 2 3/4 cups flour, baking powder, cinnamon, nutmeg, ginger and sea salt; then sift a second time. Gradually add the flour to the creamed egg batter.

In a small bowl place the chopped peaches and toss with the remaining 1/4 cup flour. Fold the peaches into the batter. Pour the batter evenly into the prepared pan. Bake for 1 hour, or until a toothpick inserted inn the center comes out clean. Cool the cake in the pan for 15 minutes. Invert onto a wire rack and sprinkle with powdered sugar.

TO SERVE: Place a slice of cake on each plate and top with peaches, glaze and your choice of ice cream.

Peach Glaze

Makes 2 cups

1/2 cup granulated sugar

3 tablespoons water

1/2 cup heavy cream

8 peaches, pitted and cut into 1/4-inch pieces

Ground black pepper

Mix the sugar and water in a small saucepan and cook over medium heat until a deep golden color. Slowly and carefully mix in the cream. Bring to a boil, add the peaches and 1 crank of ground pepper. Cook until peaches are tender. Remove peaches and set aside. Simmer the sauce another 8 to 10 minutes, or until thick and syrupy.

Strawberry Pie with Vanilla Custard, Raspberry Sauce and Whipped Cream

Makes 1 (9-inch) pie

This is an easy crust that you can prepare in about 30 minutes. One time when I was visiting New York City helping my friend Ryan Dukes prepare a dinner at the James Beard House, I learned just how quickly this recipe comes together. While preparing the dinner, an absent-minded chef let the tarts cook too long, making them far too done to serve. It was touch and go. On the fly, it was my job to round up tart shells, enough to serve 110 people. I literally ran and hailed a taxi back to the hotel where we were staying and used the main kitchen's bakeshop to make more tart shells. On my return trip to the Beard House it took two taxis: one for me and one for all the tart shells. It was an extremely close call and I'm pretty sure I set a record that day. I arrived with the tart shells in the nick of time, just as the third course was going out.

SHORTBREAD TART CRUST

1 cup all-purpose flour

2 tablespoons sugar

$1/8$ teaspoon fine sea salt

$1/2$ cup (1 stick) cold butter, cut into small cubes

TO FINISH

Vanilla custard (recipe follows)

3 cups fresh strawberries, cleaned and tops removed

Raspberry sauce (recipe follows)

Whipped cream for garnish

SHORTBREAD TART CRUST: Preheat the oven 425 degrees F.

Place the flour, sugar and salt in a food processor fitted with a metal blade process to combine the ingredients. Add the cold butter cubes and pulse just until the shortbread crust starts to hold and form clumps. Transfer the dough into the prepared tart pan and use your fingertips to press the dough evenly into the tart pan. If needed, use the back of a spoon to smooth out the dough. When finished, prick the bottom of the tart with a fork. Place covered in the freezer for 15 minutes. Place the tart pan on a cookie sheet or baking tray and bake on the center rack for about 12 to 15 minutes, or until golden brown. Remove from oven and cool on a wire rack.

To seal the crust and prevent the bottom from getting soggy glaze the bottom and sides of the tart. I like to use a chocolate glaze for the strawberry tarts with this particular crust. Just melt an ounce of chocolate in the microwave and brush the bottom and the sides of the crust with the warm melted chocolate, then add the filling.

TO FINISH: Fill the baked pie crust three-fourths full with custard and smooth the top. Toss the chopped strawberries with the raspberry sauce. (For a prettier presentation, hand place strawberries on top, starting on the outside and working in toward the center.) Pour the sauce on top, cover and chill. Serve with fresh whipped cream.

Vanilla Custard

Enough for 1 pie

1/4 cup granulated sugar or vanilla bean sugar (see page 19)

4 egg yolks

2 tablespoons all-purpose flour

2 tablespoons cornstarch

1 1/4 cups whole milk

1 vanilla bean, split

In a medium-sized bowl add the sugar and egg yolks; mix well, then set aside.

Over a piece of waxed paper or a small bowl, sift together the flour and cornstarch, then add to the egg mixture, mixing until it is smooth and lump free.

In a saucepan add the milk and split vanilla bean over medium heat; bring to a high simmer but do not boil. Turn off the heat, transfer 1 ladle of milk into the flour and egg mixture and whip it to temper the eggs a little. Remove vanilla bean from the milk, scrape the seeds and whisk the flour mixture into the whole milk, whisking constantly to prevent lumps. When all is well incorporated, return the saucepan to the heat. Bring to a low boil, whisking continually until the custard thickens, then remove from heat. Pour into a clean bowl and immediately cover the surface of the custard with plastic wrap to prevent a skin from forming. Cool to room temperature or refrigerate for later use.

Raspberry Sauce

Enough for 1 pie

1 package unflavored gelatin

1/4 cup chilled water

2 pints fresh raspberries, about 12 ounces

2/3 cup lemon sugar (see page 19) or granulated sugar

1/2 teaspoon lemon juice (if using granulated sugar)

Dissolve the gelatin in the water and set aside. Purée the raspberries using a hand-held blender or food processor and then run the berries through a strainer to remove the seeds. Warm the purée in a small saucepot and add the water with gelatin, sugar, and lemon juice (if needed); bring to a high simmer. Remove from heat and chill.

White Chocolate Banana Bread Pudding

Serves 6 to 8

1 loaf banana bread (recipe follows), cut into cubes

2 cups heavy cream

1 cup whole milk

1 vanilla bean, split and scraped

$1/2$ pound white chocolate

6 egg yolks

$1/2$ cup granulated sugar

3 tablespoons maple syrup

1 cup mashed bananas

Whipped cream for garnish

Salted caramel sauce (recipe follows)

Preheat oven to 325 degrees F and butter a 9- or 10-inch glass baking dish.

Spread the cubed banana bread on a baking sheet and bake, turning once, until lightly toasted, about 10 minutes. Remove bread from oven and set aside to cool.

Combine the cream, milk and split vanilla bean in a saucepot over medium heat and bring to a simmer. In a double boiler or microwave melt the white chocolate, set aside and keep warm.

In a large bowl combine the yolks, sugar, maple syrup, and bananas, and slowly whisk in the warm cream mixture until well combined. Add the melted white chocolate, stirring well.

Remove vanilla bean and scrape remaining beans into the custard. Discard the pods. Place the cubed banana bread into the prepared baking dish and pour the custard over the bread. Let sit for 20 minutes so the bread can soak up the custard.

Set up a hot-water bath using a baking dish large enough to hold hot water and the smaller pan of bread pudding. Fill the larger dish with hot water, about halfway up the sides and set the pudding pan inside the larger pan. Bake until the sides of the bread pudding are puffed and the center is still slightly jiggly, about 60 minutes. Remove from oven and water bath and let cool.

TO FINISH: Place a generous portion of bread pudding on a plate and top with salted caramel sauce.

Banana Bread

Makes 3 loaves

This recipe has been passed down through three generations. Don't let the loaves hang around the house too long because they're impossible to resist and you'll end up eating all three. It has to go: your friends will love it.

1 cup unsalted butter

2 cups granulated sugar

4 eggs

6 ripe bananas, mashed

2 1/2 cups all-purpose flour

2 teaspoons baking soda

1 teaspoon fine sea salt

1 1/2 cups chopped walnuts

Preheat oven to 350 degrees F. Spray 3 loaf pans with nonstick spray. In a mixing bowl cream the butter and sugar until fluffy. Add eggs one at a time, beating well after each addition. Slowly add in the banana. Sift together the flour, soda and salt. Add to the butter-and-sugar mixture. Then add the walnuts. Divide the batter equally among the loaf pans. Bake for 45 minutes, or until a toothpick inserted in the center comes out clean. Let the pans cool on a rack before removing loaves.

Salted Caramel Sauce

Makes 2 cups

There are two ways to make a salted caramel sauce. One is really simple. Let's begin there:

Place 2 small unopened cans of sweetened condensed milk in a small saucepot and cover with water. Boil for 1 hour, keeping the cans under water at all times. Remove from heat and chill well. Open the cans and place contents in a small bowl, whisking in warm milk until the sweetened milk reaches the desired thickness, and then add salt.

The next recipe is one that takes a little practice.

1 tablespoon water

2 cups granulated sugar, divided

1 cup heavy cream, heated until warm

12 tablespoons unsalted butter, room temperature

1 teaspoon sea salt

In a heavy-duty saucepot add the water and 1 cup sugar. Be sure to brush the edges of the pot with a pastry brush to wash down any sugar crystals from the sides of the pot. Do not stir; only swirl the pot as the sugar caramelizes. The water will evaporate and the sugar will start turning an amber color. Add the remaining sugar gradually. It might clump a little, but just continue to swirl so the clumps will melt. If using a candy thermometer, keep the heat at a steady 350 degrees F. Next add the heated cream. The cream has to be heated; otherwise this recipe will fail. Continue whisking in the cream until it's all incorporated. Remove from heat and cool to 90 degrees F. Add the butter, whisking quickly. Add sea salt and set aside to cool.

Sweet Potato Swirl Cheesecake

Serves 8

CRUST

1 1/2 cups gingersnap cookie crumbs

1/2 cup pecans, chopped fine

1 teaspoon ground cinnamon

2 tablespoons packed light brown sugar

1/3 cup melted unsalted butter

FILLING

3 (8-ounce) packages cream cheese, softened

1/4 cup sour cream

3/4 cup granulated sugar, divided

1 teaspoon real vanilla extract

3 large eggs

1 cup sweet potato purée

1 teaspoon ground cinnamon

1/4 teaspoon ground nutmeg

Pinch of ground cloves

CRUST: Preheat oven to 350 degrees F. In a medium-sized bowl combine cookie crumbs, pecans, cinnamon, brown sugar and melted butter. Scrape the mixture into the bottom of a 9-inch springform pan and spread across the bottom and 1 1/2 inches up the sides. Bake for 8 minutes then cool.

FILLING: Turn oven to 300 degrees F. In the bowl of a stand mixer fitted with a paddle attachment, combine the softened cream cheese, sour cream, 1/2 cup sugar and vanilla. Beat until smooth. Add the eggs one at a time and beat to incorporate. Remove 1 1/2 cups of this plain filling mixture and set aside.

Add the remaining 1/4 cup of sugar, sweet potato purée, cinnamon, nutmeg and cloves to the batter remaining in the bowl. Mix gently until well combined. Fill the crust with the plain filling first and then the sweet potato filling. Swirl with a knife to create a slight marbling and color contrast. Bake in water bath for 50 minutes, or until the center is almost set. Remove from oven and allow to cool. Filling will finish setting while it cools.

Index

Metric Conversion Chart

Volume Measurements		Weight Measurements		Temperature Conversion	
U.S.	Metric	U.S.	Metric	Fahrenheit	Celsius
1 teaspoon	5 ml	1/2 ounce	15 g	250	120
1 tablespoon	15 ml	1 ounce	30 g	300	150
1/4 cup	60 ml	3 ounces	90 g	325	160
1/3 cup	75 ml	4 ounces	115 g	350	180
1/2 cup	125 ml	8 ounces	225 g	375	190
2/3 cup	150 ml	12 ounces	350 g	400	200
3/4 cup	175 ml	1 pound	450 g	425	220
1 cup	250 ml	2 1/4 pounds	1 kg	450	230